# Praise for *Don't Print That!*

*L.A. Youth* provided a safe space for me. The old office near the corner of Fairfax and Wilshire was a place of mentorship, creativity and encouragement as I was discovering my voice and place in the world. I fondly remember the "open door" culture of the *L.A. Youth* office, made up of different backgrounds and blossoming identities, of laughter and new friendships, and of supportive adults like Donna, whose commitment to youth empowerment impacted me and so many. Donna is a visionary and activist at heart. Her creation of *L.A. Youth* and her unwavering dedication to young people should be celebrated. I applaud her for sharing her journey in her own words, and I am grateful to know her.

— *Lena Hicks*, L.A. Youth *writer, 1993-1995*

Donna Myrow is a brilliant, valiant visionary who saw the need for new, young voices in journalism. Thanks to her and her earnest students, along with parents, teachers, and community leaders, a wonderful new publication was born in southern California. *L.A. Youth* became a transcendent phenomenon for a quarter-century! And now she has written an inspiring, important book about how it all happened, entitled Don't Print That! Giving Teens the Power of the Press.

— *Charles Lewis, Professor and Executive Editor, Investigative Reporting Workshop, American University*

Donna Myrow inspired and mentored generations of teen journalists through *LA Youth,* an independent newspaper that she founded and directed. In her new book "Don't Print That! Giving Teens the Power of the Press," Donna tells the story of *LA Youth* and the generations of teens who told their stories. Reading this book will hopefully inspire high school teachers, advisors and supporters to continue the fight to protect and promote student journalism. Maybe it will even inspire the next generation of teens to see journalism as the noble calling that it is. No matter the case, *Don't Print That* will inspire you and give you hope for the future.

– *Dennis F. Hernandez, Former Board Chair,* L.A. Youth

Giving voice to the voiceless is a basic tenet of journalism. Thank you, Donna Myrow, for bringing *LA Youth* into the world and for documenting its history in this important book. Teen voices, often squelched and more often ignored, deserve now more than ever to be heard—and to be heeded.

– *Elizabeth Mehren, former* Los Angeles Times *correspondent, author, Professor, Boston University.*

There are so many great things to say about *Don't Print That!* and among them is that Donna Myrow is owed a debt of thanks for her vision, patience and skills. In one chapter, she asks if *L.A. Youth* made a difference in the lives of teens or changed adult attitudes. Yes! and Yes!, Donna! I speak as a journalist who worked at a major daily newspaper with one L.A. Youth alumnus and managed teen reporters at another major daily newspaper. *Don't Print That!* reinforces the need for more opportunities for youth to read and hear their voices in the press.

– *Sheila R. Solomon,* Chicago Tribune *(retired)*

Their stories will inspire you, and some will break your heart. So many of these voices were locked within until a committed band of talented editors at *L.A. Youth*, a groundbreaking newspaper for teenagers, taught them to weave "words to create texture, tone and sometimes, tension." Finding their voices did not always lead to finding their better selves. Some alums moved on to universities. Others to drugs or prison. Too often these voices are on the margins, needing validation, says Donna Myrow, the indomitable publisher and moving force behind the newspaper. Her compelling book is a passionate validation of life on those margins, a celebration of how far determination can go in tapping possibilities crouching in the shadows.

– *Edward J. Boyer*, L. A. Times *(retired)*

Donna Myrow's *Don't Print That!* is a unique and moving work because she goes further than to tell the stories of teenagers. She tells the stories that teenagers themselves have told through the compelling teen-run newspaper, *L.A. Youth*, that Myrow devoted much of her life to nurturing. These stories are about sexuality, faith, racism and corruption, day laborers, sex, the plight of being biracial in junior high. In a word, they are about everything. In some instances, they are heartrendingly personal. In others, the stories are fully, independently discovered by their young writers. Myrow's reflective compilation of her life's work as a shepherd of young journalists is a love letter to journalism and to youth, two pursuits which, when paired, seem to create a rare kind of magic. It is also an elegy to a time, not too long ago, when courage and doggedness could cut to the truths of the world we live in.

– *Jeff Hobbs*, New York Times *bestselling author of* Show Them You're Good

No one listens to teens. Donna Myrow did. This inspiring chronicle of 25 years of *L.A. Youth* shows the stories they hold within them, and why we should listen to them. Through ingenuity, scrappiness, pure determination, and incredible dedication, *L.A. Youth* brought a voice to people who mattered.

*– Merrill Perlman, former director of copy desks,* The New York Times

Through the story of the not-for-profit community newspaper *L.A. Youth*, Donna Myrow offers a moving and very real window into the thoughts and lives of American teenagers, hundreds of whom were changed by their experience of being journalists. I finished the book wanting to give everyone involved a big hug. Myrow's story reflects her lifelong commitment to one fundamental belief that I wish more people shared: youth voices matter.

*– Mark Goodman, John S. Knight Chair in Scholastic Journalism, Kent State University and former executive director, Student Press Law Center*

*L.A .Youth* was a font of empowerment for young people for so many years, helping them to gain a sense of dominion over their own surroundings through the unmatched power of language. The pages were written with a mixture of wonder, empathy and appropriate outrage. This book beautifully captures the enduring legacy of that accomplishment and provides a roadmap for those who might want to join in this type of work.

*– Garrett Therolf, reporter, UC Berkeley, Investigative Reporting Program*

A moving, funny, and poignant account of helping young people find their voices, and find their way.
– *Keith Hefner, Senior Advisor, Youth Communication, a nonprofit youth media organization*

A great story of teen journalists and what they can accomplish. It is a heartening read in these dark times. All I have to say is, "Do Read This!"
– *Jane Isay, author of* Walking on Eggshells

It's one thing to simply embrace the concept of freedom of the press, but Donna Myrow goes an important and essential step beyond that—she empowers younger Americans to have the freedom to *be* the press—the right to ask questions, to seek answers and to serve a truly underserved constituency. As someone who was lucky enough to become a journalist in my teens, I know all too well the importance of the intersection of timing, training and true mentorship. *Don't Print That* is an important addition to support this continuing and necessary conversation, and a vital tool for the fourth estate from the ground up.
– *Peter Greenberg, Travel Editor, CBS News*

# Don't Print That!
## Giving Teens the Power of the Press

For Michael & Madeleine,
young people have important
things to say.
Warm regards,
Nanne Myran
May, 2022

# Don't Print That!

## Giving Teens
the Power of the Press

by Donna C. Myrow

SUNACUMEN
PRESS
PALM SPRINGS, CA

Published by
Sunacumen Press
Palm Springs, CA 92264

Formatting and cover design by Sunacumen Press

ISBN: 978-1-7345643-4-1


Printed in the U.S.A.

# Contents

# Dedication

This book is dedicated to the teen writers and artists who contributed to *L.A. Youth* to make the world a better and safer place to grow up.

*When you see something that is not right, not fair, not just, you have to speak up. You have to say something; you have to do something.*

- John Lewis, 1940-2020
Civil rights leader, American statesman,
Congressman from Georgia

# Prologue

---

C an anyone trust the opinion of a 15-year-old? I believed
they could and gave them a forum.

Here, for example, is the opening of a first-person piece
about one girl's unsettled life, titled, "My Mom Is My Drug
Dealer":

> As a couple of friends and I cruised down
> an alley to find a spot to kick back and smoke a
> joint, we saw a head with long blond hair pop
> up from a dumpster. In front of the dumpster
> was an old 10-speed that had been put togeth-
> er piece by piece. Every piece on the bike was
> a different color. Someone said, "Oh! It's only
> one of those dumpster divers." Then I realized
> that it was my mother. I told my friends, "Hey!
> That's my mom. Turn around!"

The writer was Julie, whose moving story of her mother's 15-year addiction to drugs and homelessness appeared in *L.A. Youth* in 1994.

I was compelled to write this book to tell stories about the bumbling, the steady progress, and the success of my young reporters. The idea was to share lessons I had learned from 25 years as publisher of *L.A. Youth*, the newspaper by and about teens, one of the nation's most successful youth media organizations.

I was editorial assistant to author Budd Schulberg when he founded the Watts Writers Workshop after the 1965 Los Angeles riots. I marched for civil rights, protested in front of the White House against the Vietnam War, and in the early 70s my husband and I had a daughter and adopted two bi-racial children. I was ready for another challenge. My interest in young people blossomed into a volunteer writing program for teenagers. We were the Los Angeles "bureau" of a new national news service set up to supply teen-written stories to high school newspapers and mainstream media, sort of a junior Associated Press.

Every Saturday afternoon I met with my young staff and urged them to write about their lives—school, relationships, getting a job, whatever. One of our biggest stories targeted a hotel in Santa Monica that rented rooms to underage teens on prom night. Twenty to thirty young people crammed into each room for wild drug parties. The hotel tried to deny any knowledge of it, but we obtained credit card receipts clearly showing the forged signatures of parents.

I still smile when I think about the setting for our staff meetings in the late 80s. We met at the Frieda Mahood Senior Citizen Center in West Los Angeles. The director gave us the use of a room, and I hauled old typewriters in the trunk of my car. The seniors loved to dance and were soon dragging some of our teens into their "ballroom" for swing dancing to a live band.

Then, on a January morning in 1988, I decided to go for broke. We needed more writers and readers.

I was in Dennis Britton's office at the *Los Angeles Times,* soliciting his advice to expand my journalism workshop. Dennis, the deputy managing editor at the *Times,* taught workshops for high school students each summer. We were interrupted by a breaking news story scrolling across his computer screen: the U.S. Supreme Court had just ruled that school administrators had the right to censor articles intended for publication in school newspapers.

I was stunned. The ruling was a body blow to the independence of the student press. Two decades earlier, the court had seemed to go in the other direction. In an Iowa case involving an anti-war protest, Justice Abe Fortas, writing for the majority, stated, "Neither students nor teachers shed their constitutional rights to freedom of speech or expression at the schoolhouse gate."

But the truth was that high school journalism had been losing ground for a number of years. In California, the state Education Code guaranteed distribution rights for a school-financed or independently published newspaper as long as the content did not contain obscene language or material that interfered with the orderly operation of the campus. But principals persisted in trying to control the content of school newspapers, and most journalism advisors acquiesced.

About the same time, the drive to cut state taxes had squeezed funding for California schools, and journalism was among the casualties. Fewer high schools published weekly newspapers. Teacher stipends for extra hours after school to advise newspaper staffs were cut. Teens had fewer forums in which to express their opinions and less opportunity to read about issues that were important to them.

The Supreme Court decision that day pushed me to make a serious decision. I looked at Dennis and said, "I'm going to start a teen newspaper in Los Angeles." In retrospect, it may sound like a terribly impulsive reaction. But for a long time, I had been searching for something where teens could reach a broader public.

The origins of this book began that day because I knew what teens had to say. I knew they were natural storytellers. Their diaries, poems and songs pulsed with emotion. Their first-hand reports of pain, trauma and abuse became heart-breakingly alive. Their publication, *L.A. Youth,* the newspaper by and about teens, gave young people a voice for 25 years.

Unlike today's teen writers who often sit alone in front of a screen, *L.A. Youth* created a real office with real journalists ready to mentor the team of reporters from neighborhoods across the city. The teens came from Koreatown, Compton, the mid-city, Westside, and San Gabriel Valley—miles away. Students from elite private schools worked side-by-side with teens from public schools to polish their stories. Turf wars were reduced as students from every ethnic group took part sharing parallel stories and opinions of startling similarity.

WITH NO MONEY, NO OFFICE SPACE or even a computer, I gathered a dozen high school students around my kitchen table and told them we're launching a newspaper.

*L.A. Youth* gave young people a place to tell their stories. In our first year, 1988, we published just two issues, circulation 2,500. Twenty-five years later we were publishing six issues annually with a print run of 70,000 and pass-on readership more than 400,000 each month as we grew with online readers. We distributed the paper, which was funded through grants and donations, free to 1,300 teachers in middle schools and high schools throughout Los Angeles.

Sometimes our teens broke news and shined a light on wrongs. *L.A. Youth* articles addressed tough issues in an authentic manner, and because of the students' fearless, honest approach to journalism, the organization's impact was far-reaching and substantive. In 1988, for example, *L.A. Youth*'s investigative article on teens incarcerated in mental hospitals without due process prompted California legislation that was designed to address the problem.

An *L.A. Youth* investigation of police brutality in the Los Angeles Police Department was so compelling that CBS News pursued the issue further. Journalists at the *Los Angeles Times* also paid attention to *L.A. Youth*. In 1999, they reprinted a student's article about a disabled teen longing for acceptance. And in 2000, the *Times* acknowledged *L.A. Youth*'s power once again, reprinting the newspaper's cover story on the dangers of teen dance clubs. The mainstream media's interest in that story did not stop there, however; "60 Minutes" also aired a piece on the dance club dangers.

The teens' stories exposed the plight of teens who are marginalized in foster care, of teens who have limited access to college prep classes or who are growing up in crime-ridden neighborhoods. The paper's mission was to let our reporters share their own stories hoping that by doing so they would make other teens feel less alone.

I have chosen to identify the teen writers in this book only by their first name. A few names have been changed.

The adult editors at *L.A. Youth* were careful. We tried to help teens recognize the value of their ideas and guide them through weeks or months of writing and rewriting until the writer is thoroughly satisfied—and certain he or she wants to tell the story. A few stories took as long as a year before they were ready for publication. It was always worth the wait.

Alums continue to check in with me and the editors. Those that keep in touch tell us *L.A. Youth* was a secure place in their lives during tumultuous high school years. Teens are mysterious, challenging, angry and ready to break away from family to step out into the world. Some are disengaged, others arrogant, a few troublesome. Some have bright futures—college, career, happiness. Some get lost along the way and never find the right path to adulthood. I was drawn to all of them.

# Chapter One:
# Dangerous Reporting

*All my friends used to be gang members or in tagging crews and so was I. They beat up random people for money and so did I. They skipped school all the time and so did I. They didn't think about their futures, and neither did I.* - Denise, 16

*L.A. Youth* tilted strongly toward personal journalism. But we didn't avoid controversy, and we were proud of the investigative articles that our young writers produced over the years. We made a difference, and our reporters learned that they could be more than bystanders in the affairs of their communities and world.

*L.A. Youth*'s mission was to fill at least some of the gap created by the demise of the student press after several court decisions that decimated free speech rights of student journalists. We offered teens a haven, a place where they were encouraged to express their opinions. But I also wanted the paper to continually remind policy makers of the plight of kids who are marginalized by poverty and racism.

Investigative reporting was labor intensive. The toughest part was identifying a teen writer with the skills and confidence to carry out an assignment that would take many months to complete. Not everyone at our Saturday meetings was ready for this. The process was demanding, given that the teen reporter had to be willing to learn what was required each step of the way and the adult editor needed to be ready to provide clear direction.

Usually, we were able to tackle only one in-depth project each year. The logistics alone were a challenge. When the subjects of our story were young people on probation or in foster care, the editors had to make a number of preliminary phone calls and submit documents to judges in dependency or juvenile court to first get their approval. If we heard about racial tension at a school or backpack searches that seemed to overstep legal limits, we always hoped one of our staffers attended that school. That way, we didn't have to worry about access. If not, we had to follow the rules like any other media organization seeking to enter school grounds. When all of the necessary arrangements were in place, the next step was making sure our teen reporter could be available after school to do the legwork.

## Private Hospitals for Troubled Teens

One of our first big investigative projects had a serious impact on how teens themselves were treated by the mental health industry.

Joy was one of the most independent and persistent teenagers I've ever met. Everything about her said the opposite—quiet, reserved, a slight build. She had some kind of malady that required her to pack her own special meals and carry them with her to school, to our staff meetings, or wherever she needed to be. Joy never cared what other teens thought about her food or her rigid style. She and I met in 1988. She was a junior at Venice High School and hated her school newspaper. The advisor was timid, afraid to take a stand on issues that were important to the students. Joy was part of our first group of teens to believe that we could publish an independent newspaper and distribute it on campuses throughout the city.

On her own, Joy proposed a new topic.

In the late 80s most employers provided health insurance that included top of the line coverage for mental health problems. Parents didn't hesitate to use the resources available for private clinics, hospitals, and therapists if their child became verbally abusive, truant, developed drug and alcohol addictions, or hung around with perilous company. Insurance would pay the bills. Few parents had the patience or skills to handle a troubled child, so they sought the relief of residential treatment centers.

That became a profitable incentive for a few private hospital chains that specialized in treating teens to welcome troubled youth—whether the kids wanted to go or not. Charter Hospitals, one of the blockbuster facilities springing up across the country, became known for warehousing teens for up to 90 days, which was when most such insurance ran out. Hospitals rarely recommended outpatient treatment if the parents' health insurance covered in-patient care, even if the teen didn't need long-term rehabilitation. Stories about these hospitals began to appear in the news but they focused on care and treatment of adult patients. Joy wanted to investigate stories she had heard about teens who were committed to a private hospital by their parents or guardians. Nothing was going to stop Joy from investigating private mental hospitals that incarcerated teens without their consent. She wrote:

The length of stay at Charter Hospital in
Long Beach "depends on the patient's ability

to pay—their insurance," said Tari Moore, program director of the adolescent unit. "We have to speed up the treatment if the patient's insurance runs out in 10 days."

Every year in America tens of thousands of teens are committed to private facilities, sometimes against their will, sometimes without being informed of their rights, and much of this burgeoning trend seems to be tied to slick advertising and the monies to be made off adolescent care. Such care does not come cheaply. Fees at several Southern California facilities range from $4,000 to $7,000 per week.

Joy was relentless. We knew her story would shed light on the abusive system of holding teens in facilities without due process. I drove to her house in the afternoons, and she spread her notes around the kitchen table. A three-inch-thick phone book was her research tool. No Google. She interviewed mental health advocates, patients' right advocates, and lobbyists from the hospital associations. It was an exhaustive process that involved both of us.

Former California Assemblyman Richard Polanco was the teens' strongest ally, sponsoring a bill year after year in support of teen patients' rights. Polanco fought hard to ensure that teens committed to private facilities were informed of their rights to a hearing.

Fear was the biggest motivator holding teens in a facility against their will. A 17-year-old "wanted to get out, but the doctors scared her enough so she withdrew her petition," said Jim Price, executive director of the L.A. Mental Health Advocacy Project. At one of the facilities "The therapist threatened to send the kid to juvenile hall if they went to court for a petition," said Patricia Gilbert, a patients' rights advocate. Teen patients often accept the "deals" rather than run the risk of a judge misunderstanding their plight.

Not only do some hospitals make "deals" with patients, but they also provide parents with "stories." One caller to a Southern California facility was advised by an employee on what to do if her son wouldn't go voluntarily. "Tell him that you're going to go shopping—or pick up a prescription at the pharmacy," the employee told the caller.

And then a nurse at one of the rehab hospitals told Joy about Steve Sawhill and his "transportation" business. Joy called me when she heard about Sawhill and we strategized how she would get him to answer her questions about his business.

Teens ran away from home if they were told about a pending visit to a psychiatric hospital. Others refused to get in the car, and parents would be forced to drag a kicking and screaming youngster to a facility. Parents gave Sawhill permission to come to their home in the middle of the night and haul a sleepy teen to a facility.

> You won't see Steve Sawhill of Canoga Park in any TV spots that advertise psychiatric care for troubled teens, but he played a specialized role in what has become a booming business nationwide.
>
> Steve Sawhill and his wife, Leslie, operate S & L Teen Hospital Shuttle. For a price, from $300 to $2,000, depending on how far he has to travel, he said that S & L will deliver teens to the hospital of their parents' choice.

It doesn't matter if the teenager wants to go. Their parents, Sawhill said, sign a release authorizing a pickup. "We've picked up a lot of kids," said Sawhill. "Well over 1,000."

"A good percent say, 'Yeah, well, let's go,'" according to Sawhill.

The other 20 percent? Sawhill, who said he employs some off-duty police officers, does whatever it takes to get the teens there.

Sawhill was candid with Joy during the interview. He, like so many other adults we've interviewed over the years, didn't take teens seriously. Joy had introduced herself to Sawhill as a student at Venice High School and told him that she was writing this article for *L.A. Youth*, an independent teen newspaper.

A few days later Joy was called into the principal's office. He told her that Steve Sawhill called the school to inquire about Venice High's newspaper and the investigation she was conducting into psychiatric hospitals. Joy reassured the principal that the story was for *L.A. Youth* and had nothing to do with the Venice High journalism department. That satisfied the principal.

Sawhill was getting nervous. He called me at home to "discuss" the story. He was used to bullying teenagers, but that didn't work for me. I was a novice publisher, but nothing was going to deter me from uncovering the truth about these hospitals that sounded like Russian gulags. He wanted to meet me. When I declined, he said he would sue me. He demanded to read the article before we published it. Again, I declined. By the time we ended the conversation I was afraid he'd come pounding on my front door. I never heard from Steve Sawhill again.

Our reporter had another problem—Joy caught the flu and was bedridden for several days right before deadline. I drove to her house, sat on the floor next to her bed hoping she wouldn't sneeze in my direction, while the two of us finished the final editing of the story.

We published the story in October 1988. The following year Assemblyman Polanco pushed through his legislation on behalf of teen patients. It became law. It ensured that teens committed to private facilities would be informed of their rights, including the opportunity to appear before a judge for a final determination of their treatment. Joy's story documented a legal, yet sinister business of "child snatching," sanctioned by their parents as a last desperate way to control their children.

Mainstream media caught up with *L.A. Youth*'s story a few years later. "Big Business Built on the Troubles of Teenagers" read a *New York Times* headline on August 17, 2005. Investing in residential schools and treatment centers for teenagers with behavior problems is a thriving business, according to the article. Venture capitalists had identified a new business niche for their clients as treatment facilities opened across the country. Parents were always willing to pay the price to save a child's life if insurance didn't cover it. It's still big business, and television and internet ads promote residential treatment facilities never mentioning the price or length of stay covered by insurance.

## Teens Challenge LAPD

Adults assume inexperienced teenagers can't do tough investigative assignments. We proved them wrong. In several different ways, *L.A. Youth* tried to cast light on the relationship between young people and the law.

Josie lived in a chaotic household with six siblings. She

rode the school bus for two hours each way from her Echo Park house to a magnet school in the San Fernando Valley eager to satisfy the intellectual challenge she couldn't find in her neighborhood. *L.A. Youth* gave her another opportunity to explore the city. Josie liked to write and her work seemed effortless, no teenage angst.

In 1990, we heard about an incident where 26 Black and Latino teens were arrested for rowdy behavior throwing a football in the polo field at Will Rogers Park in Pacific Palisades. Were white kids arrested for hanging out at that park? Josie came to the office every day after school, making one call after the other until she found someone willing to share information about the incident. Rumors floated for years about racism within the Los Angeles Police Department, but I had doubts that a small newspaper with limited resources could conduct a major investigation.

Josie never blanched at the thought of investigating the LAPD. The daughter of a Filipino father and Scandinavian mother, Josie understood racism. Our editor, Libby Hartigan, firmly guided Josie through the reporting process, day after day. The role of the editors in all this was to coach and nurture the young talents at *L.A. Youth*, to recognize the value of their ideas and guide each through weeks or months of writing and re-writing until a compelling story emerged. It was a slow, arduous journey, the teen writer sitting side-by-side with an editor, carefully scrolling through paragraphs on a computer screen and then trying to make them better.

The nurturing goes beyond the simple editing of stories. The editors were helpmates in many different ways, especially with assignments that had an investigative element. It could be difficult for a novice to handle an interview with police, lawyers or gang members.

After school Josie made calls to Carol Watson, an attorney in private practice and a member of Police Misconduct Lawyer Referral Service, a legal organization that handled cases involving police misconduct. She represented the teens arrested in Will Rogers Park and put Josie in touch with the teens. Watson had a copy of the police report describing the incident and arrests. She agreed to let Josie and Libby read the LAPD Internal Affairs report.

"You can't remove the files from my office, but you can read them and take notes," Watson told Josie.

While Libby and Josie were driving to Watson's office someone in the City Attorney's office called the law firm and requested a copy of the files. They, too, were investigating alleged police abuse. Timing is everything—Josie, wearing a t-shirt and jeans looking every bit a teenager, and Libby, a youthful, casually dressed 30-year-old, walked into the office, a clerk handed them the documents, assumed they were messengers from the City Attorney's office, and they walked out, going directly to a photocopying store downstairs.

They returned the original to the lawyer's office and drove to *L.A. Youth* with a thick folder filled with names and dates of alleged police abuse by the West L.A. division.

Angry phone messages from the law firm were waiting for Josie and Libby by the time they returned to the office. I asked Josie if she was upset that the lawyer was mad. "I had power," she proudly responded.

Tangling with the police department under Chief Daryl Gates was worrisome. Rumors floated for years about Gates' secret files on political activists and I did not want my name added to his list. But once we started the investigation there was no turning back. Josie's story gave both sides a chance to speak about alleged police abuse.

The Internal Affairs report stated that the young men were in a gang called HRC, associated with the High Rolling Crips, suspected of writing gang graffiti, selling drugs, robbing, and fighting turf wars. The report included photos of gang graffiti at Palisades High School and photocopies of notebook doodles allegedly by some of the teens stating, "House Rockers Gangsta Crips," "HRCrips," and "Santa Monica Crips Gang."

Former LAPD press officer Commander William Booth came down hard on gangs. "If they call themselves a gang or a group, and they're not violating the law—society does."

To cover the story, we needed help from professionals—reporters, editors, photographers. The teen staff was growing but Libby and I couldn't work individually with all of them. I recruited mentors from the *L.A. Times* and *Newsweek*.

*L.A. Times* Op-Ed Editor Sue Horton was Josie's mentor. They frequently met at Sue's house to discuss Josie's articles for *L.A. Youth* and her plans after high school. We really needed Sue's help sorting out the confidential papers in our possession. Josie and Sue spread the confidential pages around Sue's kitchen table. There were legal issues—*L.A. Youth* was a small publication with limited resources and could not defend a lawsuit by the police if certain confidential information was published. With Sue's guidance Josie took detailed notes and began writing the first draft of a compelling investigation of on-going abusive and racist behavior by the LAPD.

One night when we left the office, I had a flat tire. "Oh no!" I shouted to myself. "Daryl Gates is warning me not to publish the report!" Gates had nothing to do with my flat tire but pointing the blame in his direction added a little drama to my fears.

I took the internal affairs document home with me and secured it in a Mickey Mouse backpack that belonged to one of my children. Then I hid it under my bed. It remained there for several years. I worried that the LAPD would subpoena me for the report. Eventually I tossed it out.

The big guys at the *L.A. Times* were on our heels tracking down the same story. One reporter, Glen Bunting, called and asked me to share the internal affairs report with him. "I'll credit *L.A. Youth* with the story," he offered. I knew that was BS, every journalist wants the accolades and he's definitely not going to share credit with a 16-year-old.

I called a good friend and former editor at the *Times*, Noel Greenwood, and described the situation and my jitters about crossing someone at the *Times*. His bold reply was, "Did Glen sign a letter in blood that guarantees Josie will get credit?"

I stopped returning Bunting's calls, and we finished laying out the pages.

WE HAD A BIG DECISION to make when the story was finally complete and ready for publication. The *Times* had the same information that we did and would probably publish their story on the same day. Libby and I wanted *L.A. Youth* to break the story. We moved our press run from Thursday to Wednesday. *The Palisades Post* agreed to print a thousand copies one day ahead so that I could hit the streets with this hot story. That night I loaded the small press run into my Subaru and drove around the city handing out copies on street corners, in coffee shops, teen centers, everywhere. Josie was home doing homework while Libby called the media to alert them to this breaking story.

Josie uncovered a story of police harassment of minority teens, which ultimately found its way to the courthouse and ended up as the lead story on local CBS News. I screamed with delight when reporter Bob Jimenez held up a copy of *L.A.*

*Youth* standing in front of LAPD Parker Center challenging Police Chief Gates to comment on our story. I think this was the first time the editors and I realized that the paper was having an impact outside the classroom.

One year later we published the second part of the story. The Police Misconduct Lawyer Referral Service, on behalf of the teens, filed a $5.2 million civil suit against the LAPD and City of Los Angeles citing the arrests as a violation of their civil rights. Days before the trial began the suit was settled—26 teenagers who were arrested at Will Rogers Park were awarded $200,000.

Josie reflected on her experience at the Saturday staff meeting as everyone read the story and congratulated her. "When I interviewed people, they treated me like a grown-up. It was different than how I was used to being treated by school authorities. There was a level of respect and consideration there which, unfortunately, was less common within the school system. It woke me up to how we get conditioned in school to be obedient, sometimes almost like prison inmates. I ended up clashing with some school officials because I started speaking out for better treatment. I remember one administrator was taken aback, but then seemed to get it. I learned to believe in myself, to not necessarily take no for an answer, and to keep questioning the status quo."

Our staff meetings provided a sense of emotional security where teens felt safe to express themselves. Some identified with the subject in a story and met privately with an adult editor to discuss their own experience.

Joy and Josie were not Pulitzer-Prize winning reporters at the *L.A. Times* or *New York Times*. They were 16-year-old journalists writing for *L.A. Youth*. They spent their time writing stories about urban schools, abusive parents, living in poverty and striving to climb out, immigration rights, foster care system, juvenile incarceration and everything else they knew far beyond "sex, drugs, and rock 'n roll."

Teens today with a cell phone and social media immediately react to news. They organize protests for gun control, they support Black Lives Matter, and they march for immigration rights. They need to take time to investigate critical issues that impact their lives and write those stories.

# Chapter Two:
# A Publishing Empire - Not Exactly

*I strongly believe that pot should be sold in the deli section of supermarkets because this would stop street dealing and cut down on the smoking of bud by power wannabe potheads. If reefer was legal it wouldn't be cool anymore and kids wouldn't want it if it wasn't cool.* - Letter to the Editor, Taft High School, May 1998

At first, we were invisible to adults, but teens relished stories by and about them and their issues. We started modestly. Our initial press runs were small, 2,500 copies. We ran everything from my house in Pacific Palisades for nearly two years. Twice a week my young staff gathered to share ideas, go over assignments and show me drafts of their stories.

At first, we worked at my kitchen table. But it was so small not everyone could sit down, and we moved to the antique oak table in the dining room. The teens shared two ancient Smith-Corona typewriters I borrowed from the *L.A. Times.* Some stories had to be written in longhand, and then typed out. The dining room table, which I had lovingly restored not long ago, was unprepared for all this activity and groaned audibly whenever anyone leaned on it. I tried not to worry. At dinner time, papers and supplies were stowed away in cardboard boxes so I would have room to feed my family. I rushed to serve dinner to my family so I could finish reading stories packed in boxes. There was only one telephone, and that was an immediate problem. I was making calls all day long, helping my staff line up interviews and recruiting support for our venture. My husband, Jeff, who worked from home, kept reminding me that the phone was his financial lifeline. My kids resorted to whining or cold stares to make me give up the line. The teen reporters tied up the phone with their calls in pursuit of stories. We couldn't afford a second line, so everybody just had to grin and bear it.

I was determined that the paper would have an eye-catching logo, but I could barely draw a stick figure. Paul Miles, a graphics designer and founder of the first teen-written paper in the country, The Eye, in Delaware, came to our rescue with bold lettering and a slash of color that identified us for many years.

We put the pages together ourselves, a painstaking process. The trickiest part was pasting proofs of each headline, photo, and story onto page-sized forms, like putting pieces of a puzzle together. The finished pages were then ferried to the printer, ready for photoengraving and the trip to the press. But instead of actual paste, the process required that we use a wax coating for adhesion. I constantly worried that a story or a headline might fall off one of the pages while hauling them in the back seat of my car, since the wax didn't always stick well. It happened once, and it was only a paragraph that I hoped nobody would miss.

Our printer was *The Palisades Post*, a small community newspaper. The bill for 2,500 copies was $1,500, and it was up to me to scrape together the money. In order to increase our press run and connect with more students and teachers, we needed to raise money. Friends in the corporate world agreed to buy ads to get us started, and I began hustling foundation grants over the phone. It was a nerve-wracking experience, especially since I had no idea what I was doing.

My husband was supportive of the paper and gave me editorial advice. He understood my passion since he was editor of his high school newspaper and politically active in college. My kids ignored me and had no interest in my struggling venture.

Working the phones for donations, I did my best to sound professional even when I was standing in the middle of my kitchen. I made my calls in the morning standing in my pajamas, so the foundation people on the other end of the line wouldn't hear pots and pans banging and food on the verge of burning as I prepared meals later in the day. There were some close calls.

One morning I was in the shower when my husband called out: "There's someone on the phone for you. Shall I tell him you'll call back?"

It was a call from a foundation officer, and no way was I going to miss him. I wrapped myself in a towel, dashed to the bedroom phone, and stood dripping a puddle of water on the carpet as I pitched *L.A. Youth* in my most businesslike voice.

I knew that the teen papers in Chicago and New York were distributed in schools, and I decided to follow their example. The key was finding teachers who would allow our newspaper in their classrooms. Friends and family helped me compile a list of about 25 willing teachers. I hand-delivered *L.A. Youth* to them. I thought about asking school district administrators for their blessings, and quickly rejected the idea. They would almost certainly say no. This meant I would have to employ a certain amount of stealth to avoid attracting the attention of security guards or hostile principals.

I changed from my usual jeans and sweatshirt into a business suit, to look like someone on official business. I loaded bundles of newspapers into my red Subaru hatchback, stacked so high I couldn't see out the back window. At each school, I waited in my car until classes were dismissed for the day. When the bell rang and students streamed out the main gate, I walked in as if I belonged there and delivered my newspapers.

Distributing a single issue took a few weeks, because I could only do one school a day this way. Teens on the staff helped out by stuffing copies in their backpacks and passing them along to favorite teachers. Make sure you pick someone cool and sympathetic to the rights of young people, I advised them. Over time, as *L.A. Youth* won acceptance, we were able to distribute it openly on campuses across the city.

Only rarely would a school official object since most administrators were too busy managing a big campus and I distributed papers directly to teachers. Some of my other distribution schemes were less successful. I got the bright idea to drop bundles of papers where teens congregate—coffee houses, music stores and so on. Tower Records agreed to put a stack next to the weekly alternative papers. After a few days I checked to see how many copies were left and to my surprise they were all gone. Wow! This was the answer, the best way to get the paper into the hands of teenagers.

I thanked the guy behind the counter, and he looked at me as if I spoke a foreign language. "I throw all the papers away after a few days, they make a mess," he said. "Anyway, you drop a new bundle every Thursday."

"No, no," I protested, "we only publish six times a year and the manager said you'd keep them here for a few weeks. We're not *L.A. Weekly*. What happened?"

"Which manager, the day or night guy?" he asked with a blank expression.

I had the same bad luck with the coffee houses—papers tossed out at night along with the dirty paper cups and stirrers.

Then there was the time an outside distributor dumped 3,000 copies of our paper at a school that had ordered 300. The 2,700 copies that nobody wanted ended up in the trash. Sob.

There was another problem: We were still running everything from my home. Twice a week I picked up a few teens after school and brought them to my home. No one was old enough to drive. My young staff gathered to exchange ideas, go over assignments and show me drafts of their stories. Some stories had to be written in longhand, then typed out.

Using my dining room as command central became increasingly impossible. We could work at the senior citizens center on Saturdays, but it was like trying to live out of a car. *L.A. Youth* needed a home of its own. We needed to raise money, rent an office, buy a computer, and pay for a bigger press run. With help from a lawyer, we formed a nonprofit corporation to make everything legal.

Our "angel" was the James Irvine Foundation in San Francisco, which wrote a check in late 1989 for $100,000, our first truly big grant. Right away, I rented space on the top floor of an art deco building in the middle of the city, across the street from the L.A. County Museum of Art. Los Angeles is sprawling, many teens had long bus rides to reach us. All of the tenants were nonprofits, so we had excellent neighbors. It was a small office, which we grandly called The Penthouse, despite the elevator that malfunctioned for months at a time and the ceiling that leaked whenever it rained. There was even a built-in shower, which we put into service as a storage closet. We preferred to bathe at home.

We had to co-exist with panhandlers, drug addicts, and

petty thieves who were neighborhood fixtures. One morning, we found a business card under the door with a note from a police officer, "We have your computer, please call." It turned out that our office had been burglarized the night before.

I was horrified, but I had to admit our burglar was gutsy. He had climbed the outside fire escape, broken through a door and carried the computer down a rickety flight of stairs to the street. There, he hid it in the bushes while he got stoned, which proved to be his undoing.

In 1989 I met a talented young reporter, Libby Hartigan, who had recently returned from a year-long journalism fellowship in Latin America. Libby had interned at the *Washington Post* while in college and worked as a reporter at the *L.A. Daily News* for three years after graduating Brown University. She was looking for a way to combine her writing skills and working with teens, but not in a high school setting. I offered her an exciting opportunity–train the teens to produce articles, help with the layout, work with me–no salary, no benefits in 400 square feet of cramped office space! I made no promises about our financial future.

Donations trickled in. I offered Libby a two-day per week paid position. It expanded to three days and finally five. I leveraged the Irvine grant with other foundations and small grant requests got a favorable response. Apple gave us a computer. We turned the shipping carton upside down and used it as a desk for a few weeks. Things were running smoothly. Libby and I and the teens crammed into the tiny space.

The building was our headquarters for 10 years, during which we managed to escape The Penthouse and take a larger office on a lower floor. We shared the second floor with Medical Aid for El Salvador, an organization raising funds to assist Salvadorans in their 20-year war against a repressive leader. They frequently parked old, donated ambulances in back of the building loaded with supplies they drove from Los Angeles to El Salvador. Then we quit the building altogether for new quarters a few blocks away. Now we had a conference room, a newsroom and a couple of private offices. Best of all, we were wired for new technology that would carry our stories into cyberspace.

Still, the elevator didn't always work, the air conditioning repeatedly blew fuses, and there was mold and mildew from the rain. Browbeating landlords should not be part of a publisher's job, I grumbled to myself.

EARLY ON, I LEARNED HOW to scrounge. It was the only way we could afford to furnish our office. The trick was to have no shame and be alert for news of businesses merging or downsizing. They were happy to get rid of surplus furniture as long as I removed it without making a fuss.

I hauled designer chairs and tables across town in the back of my Subaru, and on days when there was no elevator, we manhandled them up the stairs to our office.

Sometimes I had to accept defeat. When Jones Day, a major law firm, closed one of its offices in Orange County, the wife of a senior partner invited me to come "shop" the discards. I was browsing an entire floor of desks, chairs, and credenzas when I spotted a black marble conference table that could seat 25 people. It was fabulous, and I looked at it longingly. But there was no way it would fit in our office, let alone get up the stairs.

Another friend directed me to a business on a scruffy street in downtown Los Angeles. "The guy in charge is closing it down tonight, and he needs cash," she said. "He has these long folding tables, perfect for your kids to work on."

But then came the caveat: "He's the son of a prominent politician waiting trial for drug possession. So, be careful."

I took $100 cash with me and pulled up in front of an office building. Sure enough, people were dragging furniture onto the sidewalk. "How much are two tables?" I asked the politician's son.

"One hundred dollars each."

"I run a nonprofit for teens and we really need worktables. These are perfect. I'll give you $100 for both."

"No."

The street was dark and isolated, and I paused to look over my shoulder. But the few homeless folks shuffling by didn't pay any attention. After more of my cajoling, he finally gave in. Then came the hard part, getting the tables in the back of the Subaru. No one offered to help. I pushed and pulled and finally shoved them over the front seat, then drove home with the hatchback wide open.

I prowled the basement of the *Times* building, where unwanted furniture was being stored in vast, dark spaces that once housed printing presses. It was a scene out of a horror movie, rats scurrying, the drip-drip of water. I quickly made my selection of chairs and file cabinets, and never looked back to see if everything matched.

A few years later, a *Times* public affairs manager who was a fan of *L.A. Youth*, commandeered a little used photocopying machine in the executive suite and made sure we got it. That more than made up for being spooked by rats. When an assistant to TV producer Gary David Goldberg paid us a visit, she asked what we needed. I didn't hesitate to describe the high-end laser printer that we regularly fantasized about. Shortly thereafter, a check arrived from Goldberg's office to cover the cost of the printer.

We rarely had money to replace a computer that was ailing. We cannibalized parts from our "graveyard" of old computers in the back storage room. Libby was a whiz at this. She sat on the floor with the malfunctioning machine, spread out the parts, and methodically made the necessary repairs. I'm a Luddite. When one of our computers broke down it was a major crisis. We rarely had discretionary money available to rush out and buy a replacement.

Hey, if you're publishing a newspaper, you gotta be creative.

"*L.A. Youth* will be a dinosaur in a few years," said the internet "evangelist." "There won't be a need for print publications, all the schools will be wired." This was the lecture given to me by an enthusiastic "techie" who joined Vice-President Al Gore's campaign to wire every school in the U.S. so students would have access to the internet and world wide web.

Wiring was a success in well-funded suburban schools while the large inner-city schools continued to make do with one computer lab and a few classrooms wired for the information age.

Maybe these folks were right, and we would be left out of the new, fast-paced technology era. Libby and I sat down to have a serious conversation about our options to compete with the new media and strategized about creating our own web site to give the readers a place to find our stories and a way to build an archive from teen journalists.

We called three web designers and tried to schedule meetings with them to bring us into the "dot.com" era. The unreturned calls made it clear the boom days had arrived and every designer, programmer, and engineer was booked for months. Libby found an ad by a group called Cybercanics. They took her call and were interested in meeting us.

Paul Leve and Dave Satenstein, two middle-aged guys, walked in our door at 10 a.m. carrying a 24-ounce bottle of soda, wearing rumpled shirts they must have slept in and introduced themselves as Cybercanics. They weren't quite what we expected but after a few minutes we knew these guys would create a special web site for *L.A. Youth.* They were new in the technology business and understood our financial limitations, yet they were willing to launch us in cyberspace with lots of goodwill and a site that won praises from visitors to layouth.com.

IT WAS TIME TO ADD MORE STAFF. Mike Fricano was tired of long, cold winters reporting for the *Albany Times Union.* He came to L.A. looking for a job training young journalists outside of a school setting. He joined us in 2002. He morphed into our webmaster, posting articles on our site. Libby and I juggled programs, administrative operations, distribution, public speaking, counseling teens, shopping for snack food and everything else that needed to be done.

We placed an ad in journalism publications and started interviewing prospective candidates for the associate editor's position. We had hundreds of applicants even with the modest salary. Many were accomplished journalists looking for a change of pace, others fresh out of college. Over the years we've had good and bad luck filling the associate editor's position. They all enjoyed working with the teens. A few had a different agenda, we were a stopgap between journalism jobs and we offered a health plan. Even the ones that didn't work out added a new dimension to our mission.

By 1992, we had grown beyond our wildest dreams, and the *Los Angeles Times* started to donate printing and distribution. We published six issues annually with a print run of 70,000 and pass-on readership to more than 400,000 readers with each issue. The paper was delivered free to 1,300 teachers in middle schools and high schools throughout Los Angeles.

# Chapter Three:
# Writing from the Heart

*I hope I can prevent a girl from getting into trouble like I did.*

When I look at the first few issues of *L.A. Youth*, I chuckle at the way I wanted to emulate the mainstream press. Our young staff was coached to report and write in traditional newspaper style. Each story had to come to grips with the five Ws (who, what, where, when and why) and the lonely H for how. Each had to be composed like an inverted pyramid—start with a statement of the story's conclusions, then fill in the details. I doubt our teen readers found the stories compelling. More often than not, I suspect they seldom went beyond the headlines.

In the early 90s, I was invited to Nuremberg, Germany, for a week-long high school journalism conference for teens of military and embassy personnel.

I thought the teens would be sophisticated, they lived all over the world. Instead, they were just like teens at home—moody, drug and alcohol problems, rebellious. They did a good job of hiding their problems because the military comes down hard on their parents if the kids cause trouble. They were some of the most isolated youth I'd ever seen.

They wanted to write about the high rate of suicide among their peers. Drinking is legal at an early age in Europe so party time starts early.

Writing about depression, substance abuse, teen pregnancy, domestic abuse are off limits. Their high school newspaper never mentions personal issues. Problems are hidden from the top brass, freedom of expression doesn't apply to them. They had no stories to share at the end of the week.

It didn't take long for me to realize that *L.A. Youth* had to be different. We had to do a better job of relating to our readers, to speak their language and write more intimately about the experiences, emotions, conflicts, and joys that teenagers know and share.

We began to put the emphasis on personal journalism, meaning lots of stories starting with "I." We filled our pages with pieces that were heartbreaking, uplifting or funny, but always painfully honest. Our writers were encouraged to express their feelings; we wanted their voices to shine through. Instead of traditional newspaper style, our stories would be narratives, each with a beginning, a middle and an end.

Most young people responded with utter candor when we invited them to write about themselves. In one issue, we published highly personal accounts from three teen-aged girls who had found themselves facing the biggest crisis of their lives—unwanted pregnancy. Each described the excruciating emotions and conflicted feelings that swept over them when they received the news, and the decision-making process that followed. One kept her baby, one had an abortion, and the third gave her baby up for adoption.

The motivation to tell such stories is often a belief that the writer is performing a public service. "I hope I can prevent a girl from getting into trouble like I did." A surprising number of teens are willing to attach their names to such articles, but we urge them to carefully consider the public embarrassment they might endure and withhold the names when the subject matter is especially sensitive. Naming names is especially tricky when a teen's family members play key roles in a proposed story. To be certain they don't object, we often alert them that they might be portrayed in an unflattering way and get their permission.

Kim's story about her father's gambling addiction is a good example. It was certain to be painfully embarrassing to him and other family members. But she wanted readers to understand how the family suffered because of his obsession. We made sure that Kim's father was aware from the very beginning that she was writing about him. And when she showed the final draft to her family, they all gave their approval to publish.

Some of our most heartfelt writing is in response to the essay contests that we featured in every issue. The contests are based on questions like "What would you do to change the world?" or "Tell us about your favorite teacher." Once we posed this challenge: "Write a letter to Mom and Dad. What would you like to tell your parents but have been afraid or embarrassed to share?"

Here were a few of the responses:

> Dear Mom and Dad, I am pregnant. I know how much you are looking forward to being grandparents and I know you will welcome the baby. My boyfriend and I delayed our marriage because he has some minor infection which prevents us from passing our premarital blood

tests. He is kind and not well educated. He is of a different race and religion. I know your expressed tolerance will not permit you to be bothered by the fact that his skin color is somewhat darker than ours.

Dear Mom and Dad, I am not pregnant. I am not engaged and do not have syphilis. However, I am getting a D in history and a F in science and I wanted you to see these marks in the proper perspective.

Dear Mom and Dad, I know there have been times when I broke your heart, but did you stop to wonder if you broke mine? I see sadness in your eyes. Your lips rarely curve into a smile. I never saw you cry over anything except the photographs and the letter that came in the mail one day from Cambodia. What did the letter say that made you weep?

Sometimes, teens have to be convinced that it's okay to break loose and write in a personal, story-telling way—especially if they come from schools that frown on too much creativity. I'm talking about classrooms in which history reports are predictably dry and dull and English essays are certain to put you to sleep.

Youngsters in such surroundings learn to write in an overly rigid style with words dutifully plucked from a Thesaurus and sentences that read like something out of a college application essay. If they are reporters for their school newspapers, they learn how to self-censor their articles, often under the glaring eye of a nervous principal.

The irony is that in their private lives, many of these teens are writing lively, expressive thoughts every day. They scribble in diaries or share their innermost secrets with friends and strangers by posting them on technology's latest bulletin board. They write poems and correspond with pen pals in other countries. It is that energy that *L.A. Youth* tapped into.

Some of the pieces we published, like Jessica's account of her nose job, required an amazing degree of self-confidence. Jessica interviewed her plastic surgeon and posed for before-and-after photographs. Sherry, in a piece titled "My So-Called Boobs," wrote good-naturedly about the advantages of small breasts: She could hug people close to her, run around without a bra, and sleep face down!

Cosmo would never publish a story like that. Definitely an *L.A. Youth* original.

SOME STORIES MATERIALIZED without *L.A. Youth*'s involvement at the beginning. Reporter Pedro wanted to experience the harsh reality of a day laborer.

Drive by a Home Depot or a paint store any day of the week and you'll see a group of Latino men standing outside looking for work. They're willing to hop in the back of a truck to clean a yard, lift heavy sacks of masonry or other tasks that require a strong back and no documentation. The "underground economy."

"I started my day before dawn," he told one of the editors over the phone as he sat down to write the story.

"I stood on the corner of Atlantic and Beverly Boulevard in East Los Angeles with a group of guys looking for work. A guy in a pickup truck hired me and two others. We worked in the hot sun digging a deep hole and pouring cement at a big expensive house."

"How much did he promise to pay you?"

"Well, when I started to negotiate the price before we got in the truck, the other two guys told me to shut up. I see how these guys get cheated at the end of the day. When we were done the boss handed me $60 and told me to split it with the other two. No one argued. They accepted their wages without a word We were stuck miles from home and had to find a bus and spend $3 on bus fare," he sighed deeply and said he was exhausted.

Pedro planned his future. He wouldn't stand outside a home repair store again. He left for Cal Poly San Luis Obispo at the end of summer. We published his story in October 1989. Today, men continue to stand on street corners hoping for a day's work. So many of them clustered outside the Home Depot stores that neighbors complained and the men were banned.

Rites of passage were regular subjects.

We published a two-page photo spread that included a Bar Mitzvah boy reading from a prayer book, a Latina celebrating her passage into adulthood with an elaborate Quinceanera party, and a girl preparing for her winter formal.

Larry, the son of a Russian family that had immigrated to America from Israel when he was 15 years old, wanted to pay tribute to his late father. While a senior in high school, he wrote:

> One time I was alone in the house with him about two weeks before he went to the hospital for the last time. He was laying in his bed listening to music when he said, "You know what? Why don't you get us a couple of beers?"
>
> I got us two cold beers and I sat beside him on his bed It was nice to sit and have a beer and really talk, especially since I was only 15 and

shouldn't be drinking. We had never done that before, the father-son chat.

He told me a story from his childhood about how you have to stand up for yourself, a story about how he beat up this bully and scared him away. It was a cool story. I liked the image of my dad kicking someone's butt. Even more than the story, I appreciated that we were just sitting together talking like buddies. Of course, I didn't know it would be that last real conversation we would have.

Daniel was a member of the football team at Beverly Hills High School and a popular man on campus but constantly worried about being overweight. He traced his overeating to a childhood depression triggered by his parents' divorce. Teased by classmates and reluctant to disrobe in the locker room, he embarked on an ultimately successful effort to control his weight. Here is how he described some of his worst moments:

I would adjust the scale so the arrow was a little bit below the zero when I played soccer. I was slower and sweatier than everyone else. My stomach bulged out of the light blue uniform. The coach hardly put me in the game—I was simply "too big." The day the coach told me that, I walked home crying, hating myself. It didn't help when other kids called me "fat ass," "ogre," and "pig."

At one point, I was so big that it was hard to find clothes that fit. Once my parents and I spent all day trying to find some pants. It was a hot day. As I tried to pull them on, the pants stuck to the sweat on my legs. I held my stomach in and fastened the button. The pain from the tight pants was excruciating, and my belly hung over the waist of my pants. Finally, we found some gray-black pants with ugly yellow stitching down the side and bought several pairs. I never even wore them; they just hung in my closet until I gave them away.

I never weighed myself at night because I was always lighter in the morning. My heart would beat as I stood on the scale. I was full of glee if I was a pound lighter and satisfied if my weight remained the same. But all hell broke loose in my mind if I weighed more than I did the morning before. Damn, did I have to eat that Twinkie last night? Sometimes I pretend that I weighed less.

Our teen writers walked in the door questioning adult assumptions and stayed long enough to challenge our values with honest and sometimes brutal writing. Here's what resulted when they decided to create "The Teen Commandments: 10 Things We Hate About Mom and Dad (and how to change them)":

• Have meals with us at least once a week. Talk instead of watching TV or reading during the meal.
• Don't compare us with other people. Don't say, "Why can't you get A's like your sister?"

- Don't pretend to be a teenager. It's weird when parents use teen slang or try to dress like us. You don't have to act like us to communicate with us.
- Tell us the reasons for the rules you set.
- Don't tell us how our lives will turn out. We have to figure some things out by ourselves.
- Respect us as we are. Don't insult our likes and dislikes. Show some interest in the things we like.
- Listen to us instead of lecturing.
- Suggest activities we can do together, but don't force anyone.
- Encourage us in our activities, but don't put too much pressure on us if we don't win.
- Look at us and tell us that you love us.

These kids don't pull punches.

# Chapter Four:
# Making It Happen on Saturdays

*The most memorable moments for me were the weekly staff meetings because after two hours of discussing, debating and sharing thoughts, you realize that every issue concerning teenagers in Los Angeles has multiple perspectives.* - Jean, 16

People who picked up the paper for the first time often asked, "Where do the stories come from?"

"From the teens," I replied.

It might have seemed more efficient if our three professional editors simply dictated story ideas to our young staff. But that would have contradicted everything we were about—and our school-age readers would detect the heavy-handed imprint of adults in a flash.

Ninety-nine percent of all story ideas originated with the teens. The process started at 12:45 p.m. every Saturday, when Mike Fricano taped an "*L.A. Youth* Meeting, Third Floor" sign on the entrance to our building. As many as 40 young people—most of them high school students—made it to these gatherings. They crowded into our conference room and started each meeting by reporting the status of stories they were writing—or attempting to write. A reminder about deadlines always set off a ripple of nervous laughter.

"I couldn't start my article this week because I had band practice every day after school and tons of homework," explained one teen.

"I had to work late at the mall and then take the bus home, but I promise to send you something by the middle of next week," said another.

"Excuses, excuses," Mike retorted good-naturedly. "If you want to read your byline in the September issue, you better have pages to show me by Tuesday."

When it was time to brainstorm new assignments, there was no shortage of ideas. Most were triggered by personal experiences.

"My math teacher is absent every Friday. I want to write about him," said William.

"At my school, the cafeteria is segregated. The few whites in our school eat at one end, Blacks at another, and all the Hispanic kids take over the middle tables," complained Jeremy.

"I can't find a summer job," moaned Danielle.

Our young writers were getting better at recognizing how a personal issue is related to the society around them. When the two intersected, story ideas often followed.

Johnathan was an example. He grew up in the tough neighborhoods of South Los Angeles, raised by a single mother. Johnathan was a success at *L.A. Youth*, went on to Stanford University and later became a journalist. When Vice President Dan Quayle attacked the TV show "Murphy Brown" (starring Candice Bergen) for glorifying single mothers, Johnathan responded in our pages with a tribute to his mother's steadfast support throughout his life—and challenged Quayle's ideas as ill-informed and outmoded.

## Pro and Con Debates

National events sometimes triggered intense discussion. At our first staff meeting after the September 11 terrorist attacks on the United States, the mood was somber. No joking, no teasing. I asked Murray Fromson, who had covered the Vietnam War and Eastern Europe for CBS News, to facilitate the discussion. We watched television replays of the World Trade Center collapsing, and the staff wrestled with the implications of what they were witnessing.

"What's the tallest building in Los Angeles?" one teen inquired.

"Is this the beginning of World War III?" another wondered.

"We came to the United States to get away from war," said Roberto, a relatively new arrival from El Salvador.

Eugenia, an immigrant from Tajikistan, startled the group when she called them "politically naive." She described growing up under a repressive government and living with fear as part of her daily life. "You're sheltered in America," she observed.

Teens like Eugenia, just arrived from Latin American, Asia or Eastern European countries, brought a special perspective to *L.A. Youth*. Their pieces about the experience of adapting to a new land were sometimes funny, sometimes agonizing.

The editors encouraged pro and con articles when we were tackling a controversial issue. This was not always easy to achieve because the majority of our teens tended to take a liberal view of such issues as gay marriage, affirmative action, abortion rights, and similarly sensitive topics. Conservative voices on the staff tended to be quiet and polite, perhaps because they were outnumbered.

One Saturday we invited outside speakers to talk about gay marriage. "God made Adam and Eve. But God also made Adam and Steve and Eve and Eve," Pastor Neil Thomas of Metropolitan Community Church in West Hollywood told the group.

Julie disagreed: "Some homosexuals that are supposedly Christians say that God condones their lifestyles. But there's only one truth. You can't say that God doesn't sometimes and God does sometimes."

A few who no doubt shared Julie's beliefs were absent from the meeting, perhaps not comfortable to attend. But at least they were back the following Saturday, eager to write articles opposing gay marriage.

Candace, a bright and articulate student from Marymount High School in Westwood, was an exception to this pattern. She defended conservative positions with a clarity not usually found among young people. I certainly didn't believe that every Black person was a Democrat, but Candace wholeheartedly embraced Republican causes—in support of the Iraq war, tax cuts, and school vouchers and opposed to affirmative action. The other teens sat back and listened, rarely mustering the confidence to challenge her.

In the run-up to the invasion of Iraq, our weekly dialogues sometimes took on an anxious tone. "Will there be a draft," asked one of the girls, "and will girls be required to serve?"

We ran a mix of stories. Sarah wrote about the debate between liberal and conservative students at her school, Flintridge Preparatory in Pasadena, and concluded: "I can't say that anyone has changed their views on Iraq, but we learned how to accept our differences. I guess we've learned to agree to disagree."

Brynn, after journeying to a peace rally in San Francisco, wrote that war would be wrong: "Look what this conflict is doing to the young people of our world. We are being trained to kill and be killed."

Valentina, who attended a traditional girls' school, Ramona Convent, urged support of President Bush: "I do not hate the people in the Middle East. I do not want people to die. I do however, want the terror to stop."

Our teen staffers chose topics for *L.A. Youth*'s essay contests, and then judged the winners. Most entries came from teachers who turned the essay topics into class assignments, and then delivered the results to us. The pieces can be quite varied. Kenneth from Gardena High School, wistful about a sport he no longer played, wrote:

> I haven't played baseball in seven years. I really miss the times when I would just have that happy feeling when my dad would drive up to the park, when I would get a base hit, when I would catch a fly ball, or just the fact that I was part of a team.

Cindy from Hollywood High School offered a vivid commentary on public transportation:

> The bus is so creepy and disgusting. There is gum on the seats, an old lady took my seat, and a man smells like he smokes five packs of cigarettes daily and a child with big evil eyes won't stop staring at me. Oh! And there's sticky orange juice spilled all over the bus floor (I think it's orange juice).

The role of the editors in all this was to coach and nurture the young talents at *L.A. Youth*, to recognize the value of their ideas and guide each through weeks or months of writing and rewriting until a compelling story emerges. It can be a slow, arduous journey, the teen writer sitting side-by-side with an editor, carefully scrolling through paragraphs on a computer screen and then trying to improve them. A few stories have taken up to a year before they were ready for publication. I jokingly referred to them as "the most expensive stories ever published." But I told myself it was worth the wait. After all, it took courage to write something that you knew thousands of readers will be judging.

The process was made more challenging by the limited writing skills that we often encountered. *L.A. Youth* attracted students from some very elite schools, and they did well. We spent years recruiting teens from low income neighborhoods where school drop-out rates could exceed 50 percent, English was their second language, and they'd been shuffled along by the system without anyone pausing to question their lack of vocabulary and hopeless sentence structure. And basic spelling, what a disaster! It was so painful for these young people to look at a computer screen and see their weak writing skills staring back at them.

THE NURTURING WENT BEYOND the simple editing of stories. The editors were helpmates in many different ways, especially with assignments that had an investigative element. It could be very difficult for a novice to handle an interview at juvenile hall with an incarcerated teen or question a school principal about dirty bathrooms and lack of textbooks. Even the best young writer is not necessarily a strong interviewer. We found that out the hard way when Libby accompanied a teen to an interview with a school superintendent. The reporter "froze." She was nervous, dropped her notes and stumbled over her words, intimidated by the presence of a powerful public official. Libby jumped in and finished asking the questions.

The editors also found themselves playing the role of chauffeur on occasion, driving a reporter-photographer team to a story, for instance. This can turn into a three-hour, 100-mile round trip—picking up the teens from school, transporting them to the interview, and driving them home. Few of our young staff had access to wheels.

Safety concerns also required an editor's involvement. When we needed a nighttime photograph on the streets of Hollywood in a dark alley behind a building to accompany an article by a young runaway, the task fell to Libby. We did not want to expose any of our teen photographers to the obvious risks.

In our early years, I jumped at every opportunity to send someone to interview a celebrity. Our readers would love to know what their favorite stars thought about issues affecting young people. Good idea, disappointing results. The interviews were usually a bust because our celebrity subjects had little to offer beyond the same worn-out quotes that fill fan magazines. One interview had to be cut short when the celebrity in question couldn't restrain his amorous impulses. A studio publicist had set up the meeting in a fancy Beverly Hills hotel suite. Not wanting to be in the way, I waited downstairs in the lobby. It was a short wait. Our reporter, confronted by a drunken, groping actor old enough to be her grandfather, wisely dashed from the room. We left, disappointed but wiser.

Occasionally, a teen approached an editor with a story idea that he or she was reluctant to bring up at a Saturday meeting. Shyness or the delicate subject matter was the usual reason. Berley was on our staff for two years before he had the courage to tell Libby about his secret experiment to shed his "dull guy" persona. In the two-part series that resulted, Berley let readers feel his desperation to be a popular, oh-so-hip fellow. He wrote how he methodically went about changing his appearance—different clothes, a new hairstyle, and off with his glasses. Finally, he became "Brian"—only to realize that he felt like a fraud. Brian became Berley again. "It's been painful to write about this," he confessed to readers. Berley continued to write and published a fantasy book a few years ago. Sadly, Libby received word that Berley died of a heart attack in March 2020.

Sometimes we gently discouraged story ideas that we thought could have serious repercussions for the writer. Amy was a sophisticated teenager, exposed to art and culture, the best schools, and devoted parents. She wrote trendy fashion and music reviews for *L.A. Youth*. One day Amy told Libby she wanted to write about her adoring father who was born in Germany and joined Hitler's Youth during World War II. She wanted our readers to have a first-hand look at her father's hardships during that dark time in Europe and to understand why he joined this anti-Semitic youth movement. The editors worried that her schoolmates and friends would ostracize her once her father's story was revealed. At the same time, her father developed health problems. The story was not pursued.

Sometimes our writers had second thoughts about an idea, even if they had put in much time and energy trying to carry it out. Nina was a bright student at a small magnet school on the campus of a large, traditional high school. She was upset at friends and others who called her "white-washed" for not attending the regular classes with them. She wasn't a real "Latina," they told her. She decided to write about the unfairness of it all in a story for *L.A. Youth*. Her first draft brimmed with emotionally charged language that challenged her accusers. As she went through editing, her confidence grew but then wavered. She was still the same teenager eager to hang out with longtime friends in her neighborhood. She didn't want to become a 16-year-old outcast. The story ended up in a file folder of unfinished work.

## We're not always serious

We loved to eat. You could count on a chocolate cake if it was an editor's birthday or a celebration for a teen at the Saturday meeting. Libby and I vowed to keep only healthy food in the refrigerator—sprouts, yogurt, whole-grain bread. We bought graham crackers for the teens (they mysteriously disappeared when the editors spotted them in the cupboard). Ethnic dishes that teens brought from home were delicious—Nova's Armenian grape leaves, Howard's mother's Korean Kimchi. And Andrea's 5,000-calorie Jello mold with layers of whipped cream was quickly devoured at the annual December holiday party. Food was a friendly way of sharing our cultures and we laughed together hearing about a special recipe and what it meant to that teen.

Martha Stewart eat your heart out. Our special food section in *L.A. Youth* had mouth-watering dishes prepared by the teens, simple and very tasty. A lively two-page spread with colorful photos of the teens' creations and their recipes was a nice respite from the tough-love, hard-hitting stories.

We hosted a tasters' choice at one of the Saturday meetings. Libby ordered six different pizzas and removed them from their boxes. No one knew if they were Domino's, Pizza Hut, or any other brand. The challenge was to rank the best pizza by tasting them. We published the results in the next issue. The office smelled like pizza for days.

We started a knitting club. Celebrities, expectant mothers, grandmothers, even boys were clicking knitting needles. Libby suggested that we all learn to knit and make snuggly scarves. I was the only experienced knitter so we sat in a circle around the conference room and I jumped from one person to the next trying to untangle the knotted yarn and explain the knitting techniques to a left-handed knitter. Libby hopped on a chair to photograph the hilarious non-journalism exercise. It wasn't a waste of time because we had great photos of colorful yarn that months later ended up as very long scarves. The two-page spread was humorous, and we showed the readers another side of *L.A. Youth*. Guianna completed her scarf by September to take it with her for freshman year at Stanford.

The painted toenail photo spread in the May-June 2005 issue was funny and clever. Summer was around the corner and toes were on parade. Everyone in L.A. walks around in flip-flops so you gotta look good.

The U.S. government changed the food pyramid in 2005. Americans are fat, declared the Center for Disease Control. "Couch potatoes put down the clicker and take a walk," announced every radio and tv pundit. We threw down the gauntlet, too. We asked our writers to spend one week on the prescribed diet—carbs, protein, veggies, fruit, everything in moderation following the food diagram. I wanted to lose a few pounds in the summer, so I joined the team effort. Teens kept a diary recording daily meals and were prepared to publish the results in the September issue. My food diary was a secret, I wasn't ready to do the "Dr. Phil" thing by going public with my likes and dislikes.

## Postmortem

The first Saturday meeting after the paper was published was a great time in our office. Everyone was eager to see how the pages turned out. For many, it was a first look at the finished product. We would have preferred that the teens create page designs, but it was always a race against the clock getting the edition ready to go to press. The editors and a consulting art director made the final decisions on how to play the stories and photographs. Teens thumbed through the pages, looking for their own stories and savoring their bylines. Most asked for extra copies to take home. But the small photographs of the writers that appeared with their articles sometimes elicited groans. "I hate my photo, my hair sucks!" one dissatisfied writer complained. We offered to shoot a more flattering one for the next issue.

Before the meeting ended, the assembled staffers picked their favorite story. It's not always the best written, but it always had a universal theme. I learned not to interfere. After all, I'm not a teenager anymore.

# Chapter Five:
# Fame!

*Do you have a REAL job or are you a volunteer?*

The caller was a producer for MTV, the colossus of television programming for teens and young adults. "We're producing a reality show called 'The Paper'," she said. "We'd like you to shoot a short video of your organization, focusing on five or six of your staff writers. We'd also want to follow their personal lives at home and with friends."

"I'm a print person," I cautioned. "I've never shot a home movie and don't own a video camera."

Not a problem, the producer replied. Teens nowadays have their own equipment, and everyone's shooting videos with their phones. Send her the results and she would see what MTV executives thought about making *L.A. Youth* the centerpiece of the show.

Great idea, I thought. This would give us national exposure, raising our visibility among viewers who matched our target demographics. I needed to run the proposal past my editors.

It didn't take long to conclude that this was a terrible idea—exploitative, we'd have no editorial control, and there was no upfront money in sight. If we went through with it, cameras planted in our office would film confidential conversations for millions of viewers. Our reputation would suffer undeserved harm. I passed on the offer.

One journalist tried to freeload on *L.A. Youth*, with an obnoxious request.

"Do you have a Latina in your office who lives in South L.A., wears a nose ring, has spiked hair, was a former gang member? I'm a reporter at *Newsweek* and need to talk to a teen as soon as possible, my deadline is in two hours."

I understood the urgency; the 1992 Los Angeles uprising was happening. The call was so arrogant, the notion that we would offer up one of our teens to satisfy the reporter's need for a stereotype of disenchanted minority youth, I deleted the voice mail.

Movie and TV producers thought I'd be flattered by their interest. *L.A. Youth* generally meant only one thing to them—a great place to scavenge for ideas and material. From well-known Hollywood types to struggling newcomers, they all had the same pitch: "Let me have access to the kids and give me a few hours of your time and together we'll develop something terrific."

I declined to hand over hundreds of stories and donate my time with no money in sight. Someday, the right person will come along and create a series inspired by *L.A. Youth*. I wonder who will play me?

It's not just Hollywood, of course. More often, as in the case of the *Newsweek* writer, the calls came from reporters who wanted us to find a teen source. I told them to get up from behind their desks and visit a school or recreation center to interview teens.

A reporter at CNN called to inquire if I would introduce him to a couple of teens willing to go on camera to talk about their sex life! I burst out laughing. "Are you crazy? I'm not going to call parents and ask permission for their kids to go public about their private lives. They're minors."

"I understand," he meekly replied. "I'm a parent and I wouldn't let my kid go on TV and talk about sex. I just got the assignment, and we're taping tomorrow so I have to call anyone I can find who works with kids."

"Good luck," I responded before hanging up.

I didn't mean to sound totally ungrateful for the media attention we received over the years. *L.A. Youth* had more than its share of "15 minutes of fame," and it enhanced our profile both locally and nationally. Our young writers made guest appearances on television ranging from NBC's Nightly News to CNN public affairs programs. Many were thoughtful interviews conducted by smart on-air reporters, although some predictably portrayed our teens as "cute journalists." My favorite piece was an eight-minute report for The MacNeil/Lehrer NewsHour on PBS, produced by my good friend Anne Taylor Fleming. It featured a Vietnamese refugee on our staff who was dreaming of a writing career and becoming Americanized against her parents' wishes. Her parents told her she needed a career with a weekly paycheck.

OUR RELATIONSHIP WITH NATIONAL PUBLIC RADIO began with a phone call from producer Maeve McGoran: "Your stories are wonderful, and I want to work with your teens to adapt them for Morning Edition. I'll work with your reporters over the phone."

It was easy to come up with reasons to turn her down. We had no experience doing radio. Our writers were used to working side-by-side with editors, not someone who was 3,000 miles away. This would take time away from our already over-crowded schedule. There were no financial rewards to speak of. "NPR pays $150 for each story," Maeve said with no apologies for the pittance.

It all seemed a mite exploitative, but attractive nonetheless. Putting our young writers on NPR would extend our national reach. The network's remarkably loyal listeners—people who read the *New York Times* and live in upscale zip codes—were the kind of people we looked to for grants and other forms of support. In turn, we could bring a little ethnic and age diversity to NPR programming.

Our first offering was an audio version of Vincent's 3,000-word cover story about life as a young Chinese-American. Time consuming doesn't begin to describe the project. Vincent's piece had to be recast into 350 words for radio. It took weeks.

Luckily, an *L.A. Youth* alum who knew something about radio was able to help. Nova had written for us while a student at the L.A. County High School for the Performing Arts. He was a talented opera singer who graduated from USC, and has now embarked on a career as a radio reporter at NPR.

Nova was immediately enthusiastic about the idea and turned down our offer of a stipend to help produce the reports. "I want this to be a gift to *L.A. Youth* for everything you did for me," he told us.

Libby, Nova, and Vincent wrote and rewrote. Maeve, on the other end of the country, phoned in suggestions. I fretted about our investment of time and energy; would the result be worth it in terms of increasing our visibility and attracting new donors? Vincent's piece was on the air one morning while I was driving to work. All my concerns vanished in the thrill of hearing *L.A. Youth* credited on a national radio network. Wow! We're more than a local teen newspaper after this, I thought.

NPR liked Vincent's work and asked him to adapt more stories for Morning Edition. He recorded a piece about street racing and another explaining why he chose to stay home and attend community college after being rejected by the four-year colleges of his choice. Emails began arriving within minutes after the airing of his college commentary, sent by listeners who were moved by his dilemma.

Timing is everything. NPR broadcast an *L.A. Youth* commentary on school bullies just as the issue was suddenly attracting national attention. The writer was Carlos, whose poignant cover piece had described the abuse and humiliation to which he had been subjected as a student. It strongly resonated with many listeners, including one who wrote: "I was tormented every day at school because I was very small and my teeth were crooked. I left school at 14, I couldn't take the abuse. Eventually I got help and became a successful entrepreneur."

I recognized the man's name and company. He was a prominent businessman who, even as an adult, had responded to Carlos's painful experience.

THE NPR PROJECT SATISFIED one of my hopes—it gained us added recognition across the U.S. I can't say that it paid off in donor support. Each time an *L.A. Youth* broadcast triggered a burst of congratulatory emails, I added the names and addresses to our database of potential contributors. But we seldom heard from any of our new friends again, not even after I specifically asked them to support our radio reporting project.

Of all the media outlets that we partnered with, the *Los Angeles Times* was special. Our friendship with the *Times* began in 1988 when an executive hosted a cocktail party in honor of the first issue of *L.A. Youth*. What a spectacular way to celebrate, in the hallowed Chandler Room of this major American newspaper! We were invited back in 2003 to celebrate our 15th anniversary at a reception hosted by *Times* Editor John Carroll and Deputy Editor Leo Wolinsky. The *L.A. Youth* delegation included current and former teen writers, their parents, teachers who used the paper in their classrooms, and board members.

We didn't compete with the *Times*. We wanted them to expand their coverage of critical youth issues, and we urged them to include quotes from teens in their stories. I'm always irritated when I see a newspaper story about young people with quotes from a principal, a think tank expert, a psychologist, and a politician. Nothing from teenagers.

*Times* staffers, from reporters to graphic artists, donated their time at our Saturday meetings. Some stopped by just to hear our teens talk about issues of concern to young people. *L.A. Youth* articles were reprinted in the *Times*, with appropriate credit. We were happy to answer their calls for help on teen-related stories whenever possible.

On occasion, we have shared tips when potential stories were too much for us to handle. That was the situation after a distraught mother telephoned around Christmas time to ask that we look into the sexual assault of her daughter.

The episode had occurred on a bridge in East Hollywood while the girl walked to school. The mother told me she had made several fruitless calls to public agencies, asking that they investigate. L.A.P.D. took a report and then referred her to the school police. But school officials said they could not get involved because the attack didn't happen on school grounds. The staff of her city council representative did not respond.

When everybody seemed to be passing the buck, the mother

shared her anguish with a co-worker whose daughter wrote for us. "Call *L.A. Youth*," the co-worker suggested.

Her story sounded credible to me. She was worried about her daughter's safety when the holiday break ended and classes resumed. Moreover, after questioning people in the neighborhood where the attack occurred, she had reason to believe that her daughter was not the only girl assaulted there.

The editors were on holiday break. This was a complicated story that would require one of our best reporters to work with me through the holidays. We would have to get access to police reports and interview school administrators. We weren't publishing until mid-January when school would be back in session. It was too much to take on. But I felt a responsibility to help, especially after hearing that her daughter was getting injections every two weeks as a preventive against AIDS and other sexually transmitted diseases.

I called *Times* reporter Erika Hayasaki. "Erika," I said, "I trust you and know you'll protect this family when I tell you about a situation that should get public attention."

Erika shared the information with one of the editors. A week later it was a front-page story reported by three *Times* reporters. Sixteen girls had been sexually assaulted in the same area over a three-year period. The police and school officials were rightfully embarrassed. No flyers with a description of the suspect had been circulated in the neighborhood and no patrols had been ordered in the area of the bridge.

I wanted this teen and her mother vindicated. It would have been a "scoop" for *L.A. Youth* to report the story. But this was one time I had to take off my publisher's hat and respond as a concerned parent.

## Criticizing the *Los Angeles Times*

Despite our close relationship, our young writers don't always agree with what appears in the *Times,* and they let the editors know it. Ambar, for one, was offended by a *Times* editorial cartoon that pictured a gravestone with the inscription "Teen Morality." To Ambar, it seemed to typify an incorrect depiction of young people in the popular press. She responded with a piece headlined "Teen Morality Lives."

"A lot of adults out there form their opinions based on what they hear and see—but they don't see everything," she wrote. "They don't know us!"

People think I'm nuts when I tell them that our teens felt free to criticize the *Times* coverage of teenagers. "They print your paper, how could you accuse the *Times* of being biased?" asked a friend.

But my view was that it would be hypocritical if we declared the mainstream media off-limits to our writers. I can't think of a faster way to lose credibility with our staff.

Sara undertook our most ambitious effort to examine the workings of the *Times*. She agreed to read the front section of the paper every day for a month, and clip all stories that mentioned teens—good or bad. At the end of the month we analyzed the results. Few articles were positive. Most screamed headlines, "Arrests Reflect Fear of More School Violence."

Sara, it is safe to say, did not like the way the city's biggest newspaper covered teens. She followed up with a visit to the *Times* building downtown, where she was allowed to sit in on the afternoon editorial meeting where stories are selected for page one. Libby accompanied her, and the two of them listened as section editors lobbied for, and argued the merits of, stories that were competing for the front page the following day. Later, Sara was able to interview Managing Editor Leo Wolinsky, who had led the meeting.

She came away with some strong impressions of what she had seen. The editors were white, older and male. The only female in the room was an assistant who was taking notes. That day there were no people of color around the table. I couldn't blame her for feeling that the newspaper's staff was out of touch. In her view, the editors didn't reflect the interests of the community and most reporters had not visited a high school campus since they graduated.

"The *L.A. Times* is creating a climate of fear and distrust," she wrote. "It bothers me that the *Times* doesn't seem interested in taking any responsibility for this."

I sent Wolinsky a copy of Sara's story, who good-naturedly accepted her criticisms, but defended the *Times'* coverage of teens. "People want human interest stories, we have no hidden agenda," he said.

Okay, I'll admit that I wondered at times about the wisdom of saying unkind things about our biggest donor. But the *Times* didn't punish us for being critical. They kept the presses rolling. We treasured their support.

# Chapter Six:
# Don't Print That!

*Not everyone likes what we publish.*

The girl in the photograph was preparing for the school formal by bleaching her hint of a moustache. No dark lip shadows if you want the boy to kiss you! We at *L.A. Youth* thought it was a charming photo that illustrated how teens agonize over their appearance, especially when it's a big date.

The girl's mother called shortly after copies of our newspaper had been delivered to schools across the city. It was unclear how she had found out so quickly that her daughter was pictured in a feature on prom night preparations. She was furious. "You photographed my daughter, where did you get that?" she demanded.

"She gave us written permission to come to your house and take her picture in the bathroom," I replied.

"You have to remove the papers from her school. She attends an all-girls school and they're vicious, they'll tease and torment her. Please."

I told her I'd do my best. It was early in the day and the papers were probably still sitting in the school office, awaiting distribution around campus. I laugh now when I think of the absurdity of the situation—me running down to my car, racing across town to an elegant school in Bel-Air, all because of a barely noticeable mustache.

But I also understood the mother's fear that her daughter would be humiliated. Girls can be cruel to each other at that age.

I strolled nonchalantly into the school office. No one was at the front desk. I picked up the bundle of newspapers (believe me, they're very heavy, 180 copies tied together) and walked out without being caught. Mission accomplished.

We made another mother angry by publishing a photograph of her son on a rampage outside our office during the 1992 Los Angeles riots. The picture was shot from our large front office window by Prisco, as the violence spilled over into our neighborhood. It showed the young man hurling beer bottles filled with gasoline from the sunroof of his car.

His mother was in a total state of denial. "Where did you get the picture of my son?" she shouted over the phone. "He wasn't in that neighborhood."

Libby suggested she should go read her son's arrest report. But the mother would have none of it. She threatened a lawsuit and then she declared ominously, "We are coming down to your office."

She never showed up, but her threat left me feeling uneasy about the risk of some other angry soul assaulting our office. We added another bolt to the front door.

One day our voice mail recordings yielded this rant: "I'm calling to voice my displeasure about your article, 'Exploring the Horrors of Female Genital Mutilation in Africa.' On top of that, there's the dreadlock or rasta-looking person in that article. Why don't you dig up some dirt about all the other criminals of America rather than trying to go to Africa when you don't know a damn thing about it? Is that what you're teaching the young, you racist devils? What about circumcision and the Jews? Give me a call at [phone number deleted]. If that's what you're teaching the youth in America, you can all go to hell." We didn't return the call.

SKIRMISHES LIKE THESE ARE NEVER pleasant, but they come with the job. Not everyone liked what appeared in *L.A. Youth*. The most common complaints were in reaction to stories about sex—birth control methods, homosexuality, abortion, AIDS, and other consequences of reckless sex, and so on.

Interestingly enough, the complaints usually came not from parents, not from our teen readers, but from anxious school administrators whose teachers used *L.A. Youth* in their classrooms.

Libby, in a note to readers, described some of these encounters. "After we published teen essays about virginity, a principal's secretary called to cancel the newspaper, saying "*L.A. Youth* is not a very nice newspaper."

Several students admitted to having had sex in their essays—but they went on to explain all the negative consequences. They warned our readers not to make the same mistake.

A cover illustration from 1996 caused a parochial school to turn the newspaper away at the gates. The drawing showed a girl contemplating the idea of sex. She is attracted by notions of romance and love, and frightened by all its consequences: STDs, pregnancy, AIDS.

A photo of John Lennon embracing his wife Yoko Ono drew an outraged call from a middle school administrator.

John Lennon is naked in the Annie Liebowitz photo, which has been displayed in museums and graced the cover of Rolling Stone. The administrator said his students couldn't handle that kind of material. If they wanted to see that kind of thing, he said, they could read Playboy.

I remember when we were banned from one middle school after the assistant principal decided that our paper contained "objectionable content." In this case, that was code for stories about gay teens. Parents had complained about some of the articles, he told us.

We decided not to argue with him and removed the school from our distribution list. When the next issue came out, a teacher called to ask why he had not received his copies of *L.A. Youth*.

Bob Tanner was a leader in the teachers' union and was incensed when I described what had happened. As he saw it, teachers had the right to use materials that they felt were beneficial to their pupils. "Send me *L.A. Youth*," he insisted. I did, and we never heard from the assistant principal again.

On rare occasions, I withheld articles when I thought the potential damage to *L.A. Youth* was too much to risk. At the last minute, I pulled a piece on teenagers and masturbation. I ruled that it could appear on our web site, but not in the paper. The editors were unhappy, of course. I agreed the story was well written, but I wasn't sure we could weather the storm that likely would follow.

"I'm not prepared for angry calls from principals canceling their subscriptions or teachers unwilling to distribute the paper," I said. "How can we defend this subject to a middle school teacher? Every day we read about a censorship case at a school and those stories are tame compared to this topic. Do you really want to risk losing many of our readers and our donors?"

Unspoken, was my bigger fear, losing support of the *Los Angeles Times*. The *Times* was "in play," with the Tribune Company considering offers from L.A.'s civic minded billionaires eager to return the paper to local management. I wanted to stay under the radar at this potentially pivotal moment.

ONE OF OUR MOST VITRIOLIC CRITICS was a high school English teacher who declared that he was withholding *L.A. Youth* from his pupils because it contained articles that he "simply did not want them to read." He wrote, in part: "The article about Planned Parenthood was one-sided and, in fact, ludicrous. Planned Parenthood is an agenda-driven organization that promotes teenage sex and abortion. The fact they do not wish to be truly helpful to young Americans is proven by the fact that Planned Parenthood never promotes (with nearly the same amount of zeal) adoption as a viable alternative to abortion. I don't want teenagers visiting Planned Parenthood for help. They won't get it."

The same teacher took us to task for a piece on censorship of school newspapers. "Your article was effective, until you ran the question-and-answer section with students and some driveling member of the ACLU. The ACLU advised children how they might get around policies and standards at schools--policies and standards that are structured for the good of children, not lawyers. Adult authority at public schools needs to be supported and enforced, not belittled and negated. Again, I do not wish for my students to read this. It won't help them at all."

Sorry, our years of publishing *L.A. Youth* have made us deeply suspicious when someone invoked "the good of children" to defend censorship. We have had experience with that.

At one of our Saturday meetings, a troubled Mindy described what happened when her student newspaper class at The Los Angeles Center for Enriched Studies published an April Fool's Day edition. One article reported that the school's leadership class had committed mass suicide, while another revealed that the academic decathlon team was on steroids. Everyone laughed at the spoofs, except the administrators. The newspapers landed in the dumpster before they were distributed. The essential complaint was that the articles could disrupt the school. Mindy was aghast. "These were ridiculous stories that not even sixth graders would believe," she would later write. "They are young, but not stupid."

At Libby's suggestion, Mindy went to work on an *L.A. Youth* piece about student press rights at her school. She sought the opinions of teachers and students, especially those involved with the school paper. She interviewed the principal, whose basic position was that "even if there is the First Amendment, there can be limitations" on the student press. But a First Amendment defense lawyer told her that the episode amounted to illegal prior restraint.

Mindy's finished story recounted other episodes of articles being discouraged or quashed. Most contained reporting that was critical of the administration or teachers. Interestingly, the faculty and most students she interviewed did not share her indignation over restraints on what the school paper could print.

Mindy acknowledged that in her *L.A. Youth* piece and ended on a note of dismay. "Our paper needs a lot more support if we are really going to give our school a true newspaper," she wrote.

"It is my hope that people will realize that the students need a voice, and that the administration should stop restricting and censoring the journalism class."

We always worried about retribution from school administrators after *L.A. Youth* reporters wrote unflattering stories about their campuses. But to her principal's credit, there were no repercussions and Mindy was back on the newspaper staff in the fall.

I made no secret of my distress over the general battering of the student press—not only censorship, but the squeeze on funds needed to put out papers and the demoralization of journalism teachers. The situation is particularly bleak in overcrowded urban high schools, where the student press has nearly disappeared from the curriculum.

Part of *L.A. Youth*'s mission was to lend support to high school journalism. At a conference we hosted for more than 150 student editors and their teachers, we heard all sorts of war stories—a principal demanding final approval of every article, a school board member meddling in the process, administrators exerting tighter control over other student publications. Mark Goodman, former executive director of The Student Press Law Center in Washington, D.C., and other media law attorneys shared advice on how to respond to such intrusions.

THE LAW ASIDE, JOURNALISM teachers who found themselves in such struggles often had to tread carefully. The brave soul who defied the principal may discover next semester that the journalism budget has been sliced in half or worse.

One teacher told me, "I've only been at this school for a few years and the principal has implied that my services won't be needed here next year if I cross him."

Another, highly frustrated, said, "My principal won't allow a gay student to write about his experience coming out to his parents, even after they've given permission."

My heart goes out to these two and others like them. They

were doing their best to keep the student press alive, against considerable odds.

# Chapter Seven:
# The Check Is in the Mail

*We don't take teens to Disneyland.*

I always worried we'd run out of money. In fact, we came close to shutting down the newspaper on two or three occasions.

We needed about $850,000 a year in grants and donations to keep going. Raising that amount of money was a draining job; it never got easier.

Foundations were on a different fiscal cycle than us, so it was fingernail-biting time when we had to wait several months for a check to arrive. More stressful days when funders doled out quarterly grants rather than the entire amount.

The day after one donor's check arrived, I was on the phone to the next name on my list begging for money. After all, Hollywood is in our backyard and its movie, television and recording studios depend on young people like our readers for much of their revenue.

I was wrong. In my experience, a studio or production company is most likely to support an actor's favorite cause, often to win favor at the urging of the actor's agent. With some notable exceptions, Hollywood is a very insular community when it comes to giving. Outsiders are best advised not to come calling.

At every *L.A. Youth* board meeting, someone tossed out the standard line, "We need a celebrity to attract donors."

Board members called out names and I jotted them down on my yellow legal pad. I had lists of movie stars and lists of famous athletes. Generally speaking, they are self-centered, make costly demands, and prove to be utterly unreliable. If an actor agrees to be the honoree and promises there's nothing on his schedule around the time of the event, don't believe him. His agent's been working on a film deal in Hong Kong and shooting starts the day before the dinner.

I remember the well-known athlete/businessman we approached to be guest of honor at our annual City Lights Dinner. One of our board members had an "in"—a business relationship with the fellow. Perfect, I thought, and sent out a hand delivered invitation with copies of the newspaper and photos of our teens. I promised to plan the event around his availability.

After three weeks, I called his office. "We'll get back to you this week with a date," responded an assistant. Another two weeks. Another call. This went on for three months until I told the board we had to consider another honoree. Then I found out my experience was not unusual. "He's trouble," said a friend in the entertainment industry. "We co-hosted an event with him and didn't know until the last day whether or not he'd show up. Then, he had the gall to bring his entourage, free of course."

Hollywood aside, we were selective about whom we solicited. We didn't chase after government money. After all, we wrote about hot button issues like teen sexuality and abortion rights. Accepting grants from, say, a federal agency that promotes "abstinence only" would be a conflict for us, and our articles no doubt would be challenged by the agency. We're often critical of school districts, state government and local politicians; taking their money in one hand and criticizing them with the other would be hypocritical.

Nor did we seek support from big, community-oriented charitable agencies, like United Way. Our mission didn't neatly fit their purposes; more importantly, we have found that many other foundations will not award grants to a non-profit that received United Way funds.

Conversely, there are foundations that would never lend their name or support to *L.A. Youth*. Mostly, it was because of our teen sexuality articles and gay/lesbian stories. One foundation thought we were pro-abortion, though we'd never taken a position in favor or against. A few objected to our stories on birth control and the discussion of condoms. I used to submit grant requests on the gamble that nobody at these foundations would bother to read our newspaper. But they did. I carefully packaged the grant request with copies of the paper that covered less controversial issues hoping their staff didn't check out stories on our website.

Foundations provided roughly 80 percent of our financial support, and the competition was often fierce. The number of non-profits in America increases each year. Economic downturns like the recession ravaged the stock portfolios of foundations, leaving less money to spread about. Disasters like the 2005 hurricanes in Louisiana and Mississippi and the events of 9/11 quickly drew millions in charitable dollars. Our biggest supporters were outside of California—several were based in Chicago, New York, even Oklahoma—and give nationally. We usually felt the competition for grants intensified about six months after such events.

Foundations are staffed by bright, caring people who are

hard to please sometimes. Each one has its own rules and idiosyncrasies, and family foundations are the most restrictive. Some of them want visibility—translation, "I'll give you a large donation if you name the building after us." Some award grants only for specific activities, like a field trip. But their idea of a field trip (say, to Disneyland) may not square with ours.

"We do take kids on field trips, like walking to Melrose Avenue for a photo shoot and interviewing strangers on the street," I once explained in frustration. "That's part of our training program." We didn't get the grant.

Sometimes foundations gave us money to report on topics of interest to them, like healthcare or violence prevention or foster care. I also sought grants from foundations or corporations to support coverage of issues that interested us. In both cases, we retained editorial control over what was written.

The process required patience. I met regularly with foundation program officers, looking for potential funders who seemed to be a good fit. Then I sent off my proposals (perhaps 100 each year) and waited for answers. Sometimes they came quickly, other times the wait lasted many months. Once we received a check from a foundation and I thought it was a mistake. Our grant application had been pending for at least two years, and I didn't remember sending it.

I also learned how to leverage grants. If you are hungry and desperate, no one funds you. But if you have a name-brand foundation behind you, others suddenly want to be part of your success. When the Irvine Foundation sent us a large grant, I made sure certain other funders knew about it. The response was quite favorable. I was careful not to abuse the generosity of a funder like Irvine, but sometimes that was the only way to get someone's attention when you're competing with thousands of other applicants.

I never got used to the giving habits of foundations or individual donors. One year they love you and the next year calls weren't returned. A foundation that has been supportive for years can suddenly change leadership, rewrite its mission and leave you out in the cold. Diversified sources of funding was the only protection against such blows.

I am still indignant at the occasional attempt to take advantage of our non-profit status. We had a landlord who compensated us for certain damages by sending a "donation" from his family foundation. That enabled him to claim tax benefits that he would not have received if the check had come from his insurance company or his own business. I fumed every time I saw him honored at a philanthropic event, knowing how he used us to reduce his tax bill.

## Good News

But there were also happy endings. Remember the foundation officer whose phone call caught me in the shower when *L.A. Youth* was just starting? He rejected us the first time around, after I violated fundraising etiquette by asking an *L.A. Youth* board member to try personal persuasion. But we managed to repair the relationship, and the San Francisco-based Stuart Foundation later awarded a two-year grant for our Foster Youth Writing Project. I considered them friends of *L.A. Youth*, even if it was a long time coming.

Wallis Annenberg, head of one of the country's largest philanthropies, surprised me one afternoon with a personal call that our $100,000 grant application was approved.

"Wallis!" I shouted, as if she was my best friend. "How fantastic. Thank you, thank you." We both laughed.

I especially enjoyed opening the mail and finding a small donation from a name I recognized year after year. We had a few donors who always sent a check, whether it's $10 or $100. It reminds me of the $1 donation to the Obama campaign. The democratization of funding.

I learned that it paid to be nimble raising more money. All day long I reviewed my potential donors list even when I was out of the office at a meeting.

The disappointments were often devastating. Once, when a foundation officer called with bad news, I burst into tears and left the office so the staff wouldn't witness how upset I was. I didn't think we'd survive with only a month or two of cash in the bank. Dollars sometimes materialized just in the nick of time. I remember the feeling of unbelievable relief when the James Irvine Foundation rescued us from the brink one holiday season with a $50,000 grant.

At one of our Saturday meetings, we asked the teens about cultural venues they had visited in Los Angeles, places like the Watts Towers and Olvera Street.

We were surprised at the reactions.

"Isn't Watts in a dangerous part of South L.A.?" asked one of the staffers.

"I'm not allowed to leave my neighborhood," said another. "My parents don't like the kind of people downtown—they're homeless, it's scary and I don't know my way around. I only go to the mall in our neighborhood."

These kids were growing up in a multicultural city, yet isolated from most of it. They agreed they liked egg rolls, burritos, and pizza. That was about as far as they were willing to venture.

We set out to produce a special edition organized around a single theme—the arts and popular culture of Los Angeles. But where would we get the necessary financial support for this six-month project? Perhaps the J. Paul Getty Trust, parent of the astonishing museum and cultural complex in the Santa Monica Mountains. It handed out millions each year in support of arts and related ventures.

After a 20-minute meeting with a Getty official, we had what we wanted—$25,000 to send our teens on visits to museums and other cultural attractions, do the necessary fact-gathering (what to see at each, what buses to take, how much lunch will cost, etc.), and distribute the special edition to schools and libraries.

We published Howard's blunt story, "Why Museums Suck!" and I nervously waited a call from the Getty or another museum. He thought museums were boring and didn't like being followed by the guards.

No angry calls. One museum thanked us for alerting them to his complaint of being shadowed by a guard who focused on teens of color. They scheduled a staff meeting to discuss a better approach toward young visitors. I breathed a sigh of relief.

That same kind of pragmatic approach led us to a hugely important in-kind donation from the *Los Angeles Times*. By 1993 we were paying the *Palisades Post* to print 35,000 copies, occasionally 50,000 if I found extra money. We were in a rut. More and more teachers wanted the paper, as did libraries. Often, we didn't have enough copies to go around.

Every press run was a back breaker for me. I hired day workers to load the newspapers into cartons and shipping bags, all of us working together on a loading dock behind the *Post* building. After the UPS truck arrived to pick up the bundles, I went home and scrubbed the soy ink and newsprint dust off my hands and face. One night I felt a swelling around my eyes and red blotches appeared on my face. It took days to recover and with each press run I got sicker. I had an allergic reaction to either the ink or the newsprint. I started wearing a surgical mask and rubber gloves when handling the papers.

Something had to give. I wondered if the *Los Angeles Times* would be willing to help. The *Times* was experiencing a decline in readership like most other big city dailies, and had an interest in establishing relationships with young readers. I needed a media company to donate printing in exchange for ongoing recognition that it was supporting a youth newspaper. A perfect partnership.

Public Affairs Manager Lisa Reale arranged a meeting with Publisher David Laventhol. I handed him copies of *L.A. Youth* and talked as fast as I could (mostly out of nervousness). In his characteristic way, he mumbled something that sounded like yes, and we left his office. It was that astoundingly simple. A few days later, we met with the paper's operations managers, who asked us the size of our circulation. I lied and said, "100,000 copies." That sounded like a nice round number and we certainly needed more copies.

Not only did the *Times* donate the newsprint and labor to print *L.A. Youth,* but over the years its photography, technology and pre-press departments devoted hundreds of hours to improve our graphic design and color reproduction. Since 1993 the *Times* had new owners and changed publishers and editors several times. I held my breath and sang their praises with every new regime. They never wavered in their support of *L.A. Youth.* The press run grew to 120,000, with a pass-on readership of 400,000.

I GOT MY FIRST FUNDRAISING experience back in the early 70s, when a friend of mine ran for political office. Catherine O'Neill, a grassroots political activist, declared her candidacy for the state legislature. A group of us hosted her first backyard fundraiser, serving homemade food. The main attraction was Lipton Onion Soup dip. Every weekend we traveled around the community with bowls of that stuff and, as the campaign gained momentum, we made tiny cocktail hot dogs encased in crispy rolls served with mustard dip. We thought that was chic. It didn't make a difference; Catherine lost the election.

By the 80s I was helping with fundraising events at my kids' school. Nachos came into fashion. Gooey cheese over tortilla chips went a long way at silent auctions and holiday festivals. And then the guacamole craze hit us. Bowls and bowls of the green stuff at every event. I threw myself into causes that I felt strongly about—health issues, legal clinics, the ACLU, special education, human rights.

When *L.A. Youth* was building a strong reputation in the 90s, I had already mastered the art of networking at events. I could cover an entire room in one hour—pass out business cards, grab a canapé or two (especially the tasty ones served at the best hotels), bestow an occasional hug, and then out the door. It was the best way to meet movers and shakers who otherwise would be kept beyond my reach by their assistants. First thing the next morning, I would send each a copy of *L.A. Youth* and a friendly note: "Great to meet you. Look forward to working together in the near future. Hope you enjoy our newspaper."

I also learned to be prepared for surprises. Once, I brought a few of our writers to the annual meeting of the Southern California Association of Philanthropy. All the leading foundations were there, making it a great opportunity to promote *L.A. Youth*. The teens and I were on a panel to discuss racial intolerance, and we began with introductions. Each teen was supposed to recite his or her name, school and age. Catherine elaborated just a bit, introducing herself as a bisexual. I wanted the ground to open up and swallow me. I wanted to throttle her. Shocking a group of conservative philanthropists was not on our agenda. But the audience sat back as Catherine shared her views on feminist sexuality, chuckled at her humorous remarks, and applauded her at the end.

## Should we serve chicken or fish?

Elaborate dinners with VIP guests of honor seemed like a good way to raise money, and *L.A. Youth* staged five dinners. Anne Taylor Fleming, the writer and a board member at the time, was the inspiration for our first such affair. She pulled me aside after a meeting where no one else was showing much interest in our financial woes.

"Let's have a fundraising dinner," she exclaimed with delight. Anne is one of the most engaging women I know. Her enthusiasm and robust personality was infectious. "Okay," I meekly replied, wondering how and when we'd pull this off.

"There's a fundraising dinner every night in this town," she went on. "Half the people who are honored don't deserve it but their name is the attraction. We should honor the *L.A. Times*. Look at all they do for us."

The more she talked, the more I liked the idea.

"My mother will sell tables, "Anne shouted. "She's been in real estate for more than 40 years and knows everyone on the Westside."

I couldn't say no.

We formed a dinner committee. The *Times* agreed to be the honoree and I hired event planner extraordinaire Lucille Polachek. As I tell it now, it sounds easy, everything falling into place. Not true. It was the most exhausting and nerve-wracking thing I've ever done.

Lucille and I tag-teamed, calling potential corporate sponsors, nagging board members to sell tickets and tables, finding a hotel banquet room, lining up food and entertainment and so on. I screamed with delight every time Lucille shouted from the other room: "CBS bought a table, I'll call the other networks and see if they'll buy one, too."

It was a fascinating game—corporate donors wanted to know if their competition bought a table, what were the seating arrangements and what politicians would be attending. A few asked about our organization and the good work we did, but mostly such dinners were a part of doing business.

I asked alum Johnathon to be the guest speaker on behalf of the teens. He was a student at Stanford so we talked long distance about his speech. Johnathan wrote one story for us before he left for college, a beautiful tribute to his young single mother that he read to our dinner guests.

I learned a lot about a person's character when they were asked to donate their time and talent to our events. At our dinner event a local TV anchor agreed to be mistress of ceremonies, but on two conditions: we had to buy her a designer gown for the dinner and hire a limousine to get her there. I demurred, noting that business attire was appropriate and besides our program really needed the money. She grudgingly gave in.

Buying the perfect outfit for this special occasion was high up on my to-do list. My daughter Elizabeth accompanied me on a shopping trip to Saks Fifth Avenue. "No more black suits you need color," she instructed me. We had a hilarious time as I tried on one outfit after the other. I finally chose a lavender satin jacket with a navy-blue skirt. I bought a canary yellow suit as a backup.

I was reaching for the stars and thought to myself, "I want media mogul Barry Diller to be the main guest speaker." Diller was a former studio executive, the owner of Home Shopping Network and assorted technology ventures. This was an exciting time, the early days of the Internet, and I knew he'd leave the crowd spellbound. He agreed to be our guest speaker and my dinner partner. He was charming, witty and gave a terrific speech. I made small talk and asked what high school he attended. He replied, "Beverly Hills High." People like to talk about their high school years—good and bad.

We raised $150,000 from the first City Lights Dinner. Every step of the way, for more than six months, was a challenge. This was new territory for me, making cold calls to corporate sponsors, convincing their community affairs people that a $5,000 table at this lovely dinner would bring them visibility in the business community.

Libby and I squeezed out a few precious hours to design the dinner program. The dinner was held in May, right at the end of our busy season when we distributed the last issue before finals and the end of the school year. I learned another skill, speech writer. I had to write a few paragraphs for the board chair and scribble a few notes for myself.

The day of the event we loaded our cars with goody bags for the dinner guests. They were nothing like the Academy Awards gifts, no gold bracelets, weekend at a spa, dinner at Spago's. We lovingly gave a CD, a book of political cartoons by Conrad, a fancy bar of soap and other miscellaneous items.

## Another fancy dinner

Minerva came to *L.A. Youth* in 1988. She was a bright, curious teen in middle school, looking for a way out of her struggling Latino neighborhood. Her social studies teacher, Bob Tanner, drove her to our Saturday staff meetings. She excelled in everything she did. Minerva later won a scholarship to Hampshire College in Massachusetts. She used a $5,000 Ford Foundation grant to run a summer literacy program in Massachusetts for underprivileged youngsters and published a literary magazine with her students.

I often heard from Minerva. She returned to Los Angeles after graduating from Hampshire College to begin a teaching career at Compton High School, one of the toughest, most troubled campuses in South Los Angeles. Most of her pupils were Spanish speakers with limited ability in English, adding to the challenge. She read stories in Spanish to her students trying to engage them in literature rather than the dry mandatory curriculum they were required to master in order to graduate.

I asked Minerva to be our guest speaker at the second *L.A. Youth* fundraising dinner. Wow! She had the guests spellbound. An excerpt from her speech:

> Good evening. I like to think of myself, proudly, as an L.A. Youth success story. L.A. Youth has offered me countless opportunities throughout high school and college that have fostered my ambitious attitude and prepared me for all the challenges ahead. During my teenage years I was a writer at L.A. Youth and I was lucky enough to be sent to Washington, D.C. for additional journalism training.
>
> I became an English and journalism teacher at Compton High School. I love it. No, I don't wear a bulletproof vest to school, nor do I approach my job always watching my back. In fact, I flaunt the biggest riches I own, the ability to educate my students. The circumstances are extremely difficult and heartbreaking at times. Recently,

one of my students was stabbed in the back just outside my classroom by a rival gang who wasn't supposed to be on campus. The administration claimed that Karl was a walking time bomb. I knew him as a student who initiated class discussions. I've spent the past few evenings at the hospital sneaking in McDonald's for him.

Many of my students look to me as an older sister and sometimes even a parent figure. I'm the first to find out when they become pregnant or when their father has run out on them—again. I'm the first person they tell when they feel hurt because their mother was left behind in Mexico. They let me know when they are living out of a garage without food or money. But that is not all, they let me know when they are proud of their schoolwork accomplishments.

Unfortunately, there are more difficult days at Compton than there are good days. If you will, close your eyes for a moment, come with me and stand outside my classroom door at Compton High after all the students have left. You see there, up above my door where the window is located? Well, don't concentrate on the fact that the window is full of bullet holes, I want you to notice how beautifully the sun shines through those bullet holes and fills the room with so much light. Those sun rays are my students. In the end, there is only hope.

Minerva moved on to graduate school and received a Ph.D at the University of Wisconsin. She's on the faculty at a major university.

After five annual dinners I said, "No more!" I told the board it was time to find other sources of funding. I realized the time spent cajoling people to buy tables should have been spent wooing foundations. The bottom line was the same at the end of the next fiscal year when we didn't have a dinner and I didn't collapse from exhaustion.

## Money chase continues

My best night on the dinner circuit was an event at the Century City Hotel for a legal assistance organization. I networked during the cocktail hour and silent auction. When it was time for the sit-down dinner. I looked around the ballroom at hundreds of guests and Cornish Hens stuffed with wild rice at every place setting and wanted out. I was tired after a long day at work. I rode the escalator to the lobby, music was coming from the patio. It was a warm summer night so I wandered in that direction. A jazz band was playing, people were dancing and "food stations" offered Mexican, Thai, Italian and every other ethnic cuisine. This looked like a lot more fun than the event I had just left.

"Hi, my name's Bill and I'm a sales rep from the Midwest," said the man in a blue blazer and tan pants who walked up to greet me.

"Donna," I said, "and I live here in L.A."

He clearly assumed I belonged there, and I did not dissuade him. "What a gorgeous night for an outdoor party," I observed brightly. "I'll be right back, I want to get a glass of wine."

As I made my way to the bar, a drum roll stopped all conversation and an enthusiastic fellow stood to make an announcement. "It's time for the raffle drawing, so hold on to your tickets," he shouted into the microphone.

I looked down at the closest table and there was a cluster of red raffle tickets that someone had left behind. Naturally, I picked them up. Just like in the movies, I won two free dinners to a famous Beverly Hills restaurant.

On my way out, someone handed me a sack full of trinkets from the poshest of shops—an honest-to-goodness "goodie bag." Fundraising nights should always be like this.

I'M FREQUENTLY ASKED HOW MUCH support we got from the entertainment industry and I shook my head and shrugged my shoulders. "Very little money, which is frustrating since they're in our own backyard." Their generosity was insular, a studio or production company gives to an actor's favorite cause or an agent's client. Outsiders beware, don't come calling. One entertainment giant gave us a $5,000 donation. I guess we angered them when we sent two reporters to the opening day of their new theme park and published a story that described the two-hour search for their car in the vast parking lot and how expensive it would be for teens. The teens did write about the fun rides. We never received a donation from them after that story.

On July 1 every year, I started over raising money to pay salaries, rent, program expenses, etc. There were few multi-year grants after the foundation stock portfolios took a big hit from the 2008 recession.

I loved to open the mail and find a small donation from a name I recognized year after year. We had a few donors who always send a check, whether it was $10 or $100.

Our board members joined our team for a variety of reasons—some want to make a difference in the community or their company encourages volunteerism and networking for business contacts. One of our requirements to join the board was to raise money. But very few board members are comfortable asking colleagues, friends or family members for money.

No one likes to ask for money—especially me. Some members solicit donations from their employer or business partners and others write a personal check every year.

There was a period in the mid-90s when the economy was strong and fundraising was easier. My board had 25 members, senior and mid-level executives. The meetings were fun and bringing in corporate dollars was not such an onerous task. L.A. still had a few Fortune 500 companies, ARCO, Bank of America. The technology boom was in Northern California but the burgeoning internet and ancillary products enabled local businesses to expand their market.

People are attracted to the media. Being connected to an organization that publishes a newspaper is different than sitting on a board of a hospital, a cultural center or the local YMCA. The "suits" liked to reminisce about their high school or college days writing for the student newspaper, protesting student fee hikes and lack of parking spaces or writing an editorial in favor of affirmative action. They liked to hear my stories about investigative reporting, shaking up the system. It was a memory rush when they did the same thing.

# Chapter Eight:
# The Outcasts—Life on the Margins

---

*Skid Row was like living in a madhouse. There'd be people
walking down the hallway talking to themselves. Some would go
weeks or months without taking a bath. That's not normal. You
go on one floor and it smells okay, then you go on another floor
and it smells like somebody died.* — Anonymous, 16

Our readership expanded when more teachers requested
copies. Our journalism got better with each issue, but
something didn't feel right. *L.A. Youth* was not reaching out
to the neediest teens. We had to build relationships with three
overlooked groups:

• Young people living on the streets. They lived with
trauma and violence on a daily basis, often selling themselves
into prostitution and becoming addicted to drugs. They were
so marginalized that no one gave them a second thought.

• The hundreds of children in foster care moving in and
out of group homes or other shelters. Most were refugees from
abusive or broken families. Some were so emotionally scarred
that they retreated into silence.

• Teens afflicted with various mental disorders. The lucky
ones had parents able to afford therapists, medications, and
special schooling.

• Others, including those who found themselves on the streets or funneled into foster care, might or might not receive appropriate treatment.

WE SET OUT TO FIND WRITERS in the three groups whose first-person stories would convey the reality of their lives. Our intent was to influence policy makers with the power to improve services for these teens, and to remind the mainstream media that they existed. It was an effort that would be rife with problems, even after months of careful planning.

I met with a program officer at The California Endowment to discuss expanding our outreach to teens in foster care and the juvenile justice system. The foundation expressed interested and suggested I apply for a grant to hire another editor and funds to support additional expenses.

We launched the Foster Youth Writing Project in 2003 and hired Amanda Riddle, a reporter at the Associated Press with enormous amounts of patience and eager to bring her journalism experience to *L.A. Youth.*

Many of these young people had been so neglected or abandoned that they did not trust adults. Their writing skills were often poor, some had anger management problems, and many were serial runaways. Their attention spans typically were 20 minutes or less. Their stories usually required repeated and intense editing sessions stretching over many months.

There were kids like Chance, who ran away from his 20th group home to search for his mother in Las Vegas. We were told his mother was a prostitute and a drug addict. Chance imagined that if he found her, she'd be thrilled to see him and the two of them could live together happily ever after. Isn't that how fairy tales end?

Gar left her home in Utah when she was 13 and wandered

back and forth between shelters and the streets of Hollywood for the next five years. One of our editors met her at a shelter, and out of that encounter came a harrowing essay entitled "Homeless for the Holidays." Gar wrote:

> It was about four years ago Christmas day, and I awoke out of a deep, dreamless, and much needed sleep on Hollywood Boulevard behind the Egyptian Theater. I lay curled up inside my blanket, the only shield that separated me from the dirt and rocks on the ground. The theater was under construction at the time, so from the outside the place looked like the aftermath of a tornado. To me, it was home.
>
> Tucked behind a wall to the theater, I felt semi-safe. A fence hid it. The cops never came there. Not a bad deal for a 15-year-old living on her own.
>
> Sunlight danced on my face, and I rubbed my eyes, I felt insanely tired, like most mornings, because most nights I woke up at least 10 times to make sure nobody found me. I always slept with my back to the wall and my knife on my belt, just in case.

Gar became the subject of a profile in the *Los Angeles Times*, after City Editor Bill Boyarsky saw the *L.A. Youth* piece and assigned a reporter to spend time with her as she moved from the shelter back to the streets and ultimately to another city. Later, Gar asked us for a letter of recommendation to accompany her application to join the military. We didn't have much hope for a girl who was used to living on the streets suddenly following anyone's orders. Months later, we heard that she had left the military after boot camp.

## A World Apart

Amanda, the lead editor for most of our outreach effort, found teens living in dilapidated hotels or shelters on Skid Row, the area of downtown Los Angeles strewn with trash, drug users, and the homeless. Many had gone there with parents who had fallen on hard times and could not afford anything better. Even so, these youngsters often exhibited a startling resilience.

The teen writer had been one of them, spending four years on Skid Row before making her escape. She wrote:

> How do kids end up on Skid Row? I had been living in South L.A. with my mom and older brother and sister. For me, it started with my mom's drug problem at the beginning of seventh grade. All of a sudden, we didn't have hot water or gas. On New Year's Day 2000, my mom woke me up and said we would be staying with some relatives. From there we moved around a lot until we had nowhere to go.
>
> In June, we moved to the Union Rescue Mission, a homeless shelter on Skid Row. I'd never seen a place like Skid Row before. There were a lot of homeless people just out and about. You walked down the street and saw tents and cardboard boxes blocking the sidewalk, people selling drugs or cigarettes, other people sleeping on the sidewalk. People walking with a 40-ounce beer in their hand. You walk down the street and out of

nowhere someone starts talking to you or cusses you out or you see people talking to themselves. I wasn't scared, but it made me nervous.

She and her family found a room in a Skid Row hotel.

The first night I was scared because I saw a cockroach two inches long. All four of us slept in a king-sized bed. The only other piece of furniture was an old, rusty brown cabinet. Then we got furniture from other people's rooms when they moved out. We bought a hot plate, and someone gave us a refrigerator. We got our TV, VCR, and pictures from our relative's house. But it still didn't feel like home.

Living in the hotel was a mystery. Often, the electricity would go out for a few hours or they would shut the water off without notice. Sometimes, floors would flood and the fire department would come.

It was like living in a madhouse. There'd be people walking down the hallway talking to themselves. Some would go weeks or months without taking a bath. That's not normal. You go on one floor and it smells OK, then you go on another floor and it smells like somebody died.

At first, there were only a few other kids in the hotel. One kid had been living in a house, but his dad couldn't pay the mortgage. Another kid's house had burned down.

After her piece was completed, we didn't hear from her for more than a month. Then one day she appeared in the office, wearing baggy sweatpants and a snug T-shirt barely covering her round stomach.

"Oh, no," I thought.

She announced that she was pregnant, no mention of the father, and we collectively sighed and hugged her. She was living in a shelter for homeless and runaway youth but needed to relocate. We gave her information on shelters for pregnant teens and reminded her to get pre-natal care. There was nothing else we could do.

I found the girl from Skid Row in 2020. It had been 14 years since we spoke, but my outreach efforts to alums via the internet is bringing us together. She lives in a neighborhood far from downtown L.A. as a single mother with three children. Life is tough without a full-time job, and she has loans from classes at a private vocational school. But she's safe and in good spirits. We promised to meet once the pandemic is over.

To CONNECT WITH TEENS in foster care, Amanda worked with social workers, group homes, judges, and others. One of her recruits was William, who wrote this matter-of-fact explanation of how it all began for him:

> When I was a little kid, I would stay out as long as I could around my neighborhood and at the park to avoid getting beat by my dad. When I was 5, my dad burned me on the stove, and I was put into foster care.

He described years of moving in and out of group homes, constantly running away, and finally taking to the streets as a teenager, panhandling to survive and living in a city park.

I started doing crack cocaine and other drugs like crystal meth, coke, and speed. At night I would sleep in the jungle gym, in the slide that was a tube, because it was warmer. When it rained I would sleep under the freeway. Once in a while I could get a good night's sleep. But other nights I couldn't because I was worried about getting caught by the police. Every now and then I would hear gunfire and it would keep me up at night.

My clothes were dirty and ripped. I smelled like piss and body odor. I would eat out of garbage cans or steal food. Before I started living on the street, I was a good 135 pounds. I lost a lot of weight. I looked like a twig. I would go a few days without eating. For the first couple days I would be starving, but on the third day the hunger went away, and I couldn't feel anything.

He burglarized houses to support his drug habit, and eventually was arrested and placed in a locked-down group home. He emerged "older and wiser," as he put it.

For the first time, I have plans for the future. I want to go to a trade school to learn roofing. I also want to get my own place soon. Then I'll have all the freedom I want. I know I won't return to drugs. I know what I have to do to survive. I'm going to get a job and be somebody.

Staying in touch with William, as with others like him, was always difficult. But one afternoon he called after seeing his published story online at a cybercafé and came by the office to pick up the $100 stipend we were holding for him. Teens in foster care were eligible for a $100 stipend provided by a foundation grant. He had turned 18 and, as a former foster care child, was eligible for so-called transitional housing in an apartment. But he passed it up and slept in his car instead. William hated everything associated with the foster care system and wanted nothing more to do with it.

### Voices No One Else Can Hear

Sixteen-year-old Brian was a big, cheerful guy with short cropped blond hair and a red flush across his pale cheeks. He liked to snack on our supply of graham crackers, always with a huge glob of peanut butter on top. Amanda met him on one of her weekly visits to the Linden Center, a private school for youngsters with emotional and behavioral problems. He had an unusual story to tell. He heard voices.

> Before I was 10, I lived pretty much a normal life. I had fun with my friends. I played outside in the street and slept over at their houses. All that stopped when I was in the fifth grade. The voices told me to kill myself or kill others. One day I was in the kitchen when I spaced out for a few minutes—I was standing there like a zombie. I was holding a knife to my stomach. My mom came in and saw me and persuaded me to put it down. My parents called the police, who came and told me to put the knife down.

I got scared at that point. I went to the hospital for a week. I was in and out of the hospital for the next year.

The doctors recommended that I go to a group home where I would live with adult staff members and five other boys who were in foster care or had emotional problems. I thought it would be better for me because I could get help 24/7.

Therapy has also helped me communicate when I'm hearing voices. In June when I heard voices in class I was surprised. They were chanting the word "hate." It was the Tuesday before Father's Day. I wanted to go home and cook my dad breakfast. But I couldn't go home because I was on safety restriction at the group home. That's when you can't go out by yourself or have anything sharp. Instead, my parents came and saw me for four hours, and I gave my dad a card.

I'm getting better. I'm not taking as many meds. I'm hopeful I'm going to make it in life. I want to get a job. I think I'll be able to handle my depression if I hear voices.

As he worked on his story, Brian was able to spend time at home with his family. But shortly before the final draft was completed, he had a breakdown and was briefly hospitalized. When his piece finally appeared in *L.A. Youth*, he visited our office. He was proud to see his story in print and wanted extra copies for his classmates.

Batya was also recruited from the Linden Center. She was a pretty girl with brown hair and blue eyes and a complicated childhood. Born to a drug addict, she was placed in foster care until adoption at age two by a strict religious family. The young Batya was combative with her parents, teachers, therapists, everyone in her life. She bounced from one special education program to the next, until finally her parents sent her to a locked-down facility in Utah that specialized in hard-to-handle teens. She was there for two years, then returned home, still a very troubled girl.

Batya was always hungry and approached food with a certain abandon. On weekly visits to our office, her favorite lunch was sushi rolls, iced cappuccino, and cookies, which she bought at a nearby convenience store during editing breaks.

For 10 months, she wrote and re-wrote her story, mainly an account of her time in Utah. Her attendance was sporadic, and one month before her 18th birthday, she stopped coming. She had run away from home and disappeared. After several weeks without hearing from Batya, we decided to publish her story the way she had left it. In part, it read:

> When I was nine, I found out I was adopted. My biological mother was a prostitute and drug addict. When she was pregnant with me, she continued to do drugs. When I was born, I had a chemical imbalance in my brain.
>
> I was 12 when my mom and dad pulled me into my dad's office and told me they were sending me to a school in Utah. My parents told me my behavior was dangerous and they thought the school would change me for the better.

Before coming to Utah, I had started fires, locked family members in rooms, stole, lied, had sexual relationships with boys, ran away, got into fights, was abusive toward people, and tried to commit suicide a couple times.

Therapists have labeled me "out of control" and "emotionally disturbed." I didn't know it at the time, but before I left for Utah, I would have to look back at what I had done that got me here.

I've spent a lot of time ruining my family's life. Looking back, I wish I had a rewind button. I didn't want to change because I was more comfortable in the behavior I was used to. But now I see things better. I'm thankful my family gave me the chance to change.

Readers voiced their appreciation of the story in thoughtful letters and emails. A month later, Batya walked into our office. I thought she might be displeased that we had gone ahead and printed the story in her absence, but she was not. She just wanted to visit and pick up some extra copies of the issue.

"I'm engaged and getting married this summer in Paris," she exclaimed. She had met her husband-to-be "at this place in Hollywood, and we moved to his apartment. He's 20 and he loves me."

Batya hadn't graduated from high school, let alone prepared for a trip to Paris. She said she was working in a bakery but couldn't remember its name or location. She finally had to admit that she lost her bus pass and didn't have money to get home. We gave her a few dollars, told her to keep in touch and out the door she went.

Months later, searching the internet for missing alums, we came across a provocative photo of Batya in a pink bra and low-slung jeans with a tattooed cross on her arm and a sullen look on her face. Her boyfriend had posted the photo together with a request that anyone who knew her should tell Batya to come and get the three bags she left behind.

We all stared at the photo. There wasn't much to say.

And then she reappeared, looking older than her 19 years, with stringy blonde hair and sunken eyes rimmed with dark circles. She wore a torn, dirty sweatshirt and baggy pants three sizes too large for her noticeably thinner body.

"We missed you," I said, delighted to see Batya again.

"I got married. I stayed with my mother when I got the flu. Today I'm staying with my friend Christine because my mother and I had an argument. I have herpes, so I'm taking medication. I bleached my hair. You can see the dark roots. I'm looking for a job."

The words spilled out without a pause. The room was quiet for a few seconds, while we tried to absorb all she had said. "I want to come back and write another story," she added.

Our policy was to allow alums to contribute stories until they were 20 years old, and we had always been fond of Batya. We happily agreed.

"Okay," she said. "I'll see you soon."

After she left, we speculated on whether she was homeless or back on drugs. She seemed to have gone a while without bathing. Libby had noticed Batya rubbing her hand across her stomach and wondered if she were pregnant.

I felt a lump in my throat. I'm the boss, I can't cry in front of the staff over a teenager, I thought. "How will she survive?" I said to no one in particular.

Batya never came back. I sometimes wonder if she is still alive.

WE CAME TO KNOW A NUMBER of teens like Batya, full of desire to express themselves in writing but with lives in such disorder that their stories were often left half-finished or not even started.

Cavanaff was one of those. She was raised by foster parents until age 11, when social workers found that she was being abused and placed her in a group home. She became a runaway and was arrested for prostitution. She was confined to juvenile hall more than once and went in and out of other group homes and shelters.

After starting to work with Amanda on the story of her life, she disappeared for a time. Then came an email: "I'm staying with friends, five months pregs and tomorrow I'm 18. I want to finish my story, so I'll come to the office."

Cavanaff arrived in a state of distress. Her t-shirt read, "Smile, Smile, Have a Happy Day," but she was tearful and frantic about the "mess" that her life had become. Her immediate problem was how to get to a shelter for pregnant teenagers by nightfall. It was in an adjoining county, and she was $3 short of the $9 needed to buy a train ticket.

Amanda and I gave her hugs, sat her down in a chair and promised to help. I handed her $50, enough for the ticket with something left over for other needs. Libby filled a tote bag with a quilt and toiletries from our earthquake kit and put it in her hands.

Then I drove Cavanaff to the train station. On the way, she shared some grim secrets. Her pimp had fathered the baby. When she finally sought pre-natal care, she learned that she had a sexually transmitted disease, vaginal warts.

I took a deep breath, tears welled in my eyes and I could barely look at her. I needed to think happy thoughts. "I'm going to be a grandmother today or tomorrow," I told her. "My

**Teen art for an *L.A. Youth* cover story on teen depression.**

son and his wife are having a third boy." She turned to me and smiled without a word.

At the train station, we said our goodbyes, and I watched her hurry inside. I drove away filled with sadness. Two babies coming into the world—my grandchild, secure with family, friends, all the loving support a baby would need, and the other entering the world in the arms of a teenage mother without a friend or family member by her side.

Three months later, she was back in Los Angeles for a final appearance in juvenile court. This time it was to complete her emancipation from the foster care system. All went well, and a month afterwards a baby girl arrived. Amanda mailed a supply of diapers and a blanket to the address where Cavanaff was now living with a man she had met over the internet.

Going through my files recently, I found an all-caps note she had sent when eight months pregnant. She had enclosed photographs of her swollen belly, and seemed full of optimism after qualifying for an assistance program:

> WELL I GOT MY BENEFITS THE WHOLE NINE YARD!!!!!!!!!!!!!!
> I CAN FINALLY FEEL LIKE I CAN SURVIVE! FOR ME AND MY BABY
> TO GET ME OFF MY FEET AND GET A REGULAR JOB!
> I SENT THOSE PICS YOU CAN DISPOSE OF THEM BUT I WANTED YOU TO SEE HOW HAPPY THIS PREGNANCY HAS CHANGED ME SORRY ABOUT THE (NOT SO CLOTHED I'M JUST VERY HAPPY I DID NT GET AN ABORTION) THANK YOU AMANDA FOR THE HOPE AND SUPPORT BECAUSE THERE NOT ALOT OF PEOPLE LIKE YOU AND YOUR COMPANY LA YOUTH ITS BUILT ALOT IN ME I DIDN'T HAVE BEFORE I KNEW ALL YA EDITORS YOU GIVE ME FAITH THAT I CAN BE SOMEBODY AND MORE THEN A STATISTIC .

The first draft of her *L.A. Youth* story ended up in our unfinished file. It would require a lot more work before being ready to print, and Cavanaff's life was simply too chaotic to allow that. After becoming a mother, she told a counselor she was worried about money, finding a job, and finding permanent housing. Sometimes, she confided, "I get so frustrated I could throw the baby against a wall!"

The counselor called child protective services and police, and the baby was put in temporary foster care. No happy endings for Cavanaff, it seems.

## Working in the System

I will admit that my commitment to outreach was sometimes put to the test, especially by the juvenile justice system. Dealing with it required endless amounts of patience and an inexhaustible tolerance for bureaucratic idiosyncrasies.

When one of our teen reporters wanted to interview a youngster in juvenile hall, we couldn't just pick up the phone and inquire about a convenient time to visit. Adult reporters have that freedom. Because our reporters are teenagers, we had to petition the probation department for permission. Back and forth documents streamed through the fax machine. It took weeks. Finally, the approval arrived, and we were able to proceed with the interview.

Soliciting articles from teens in the system was chancy. We had good experiences, like the day Mike spent time at a remote mountain camp for juvenile offenders. At the invitation of their teacher, he guided several youngsters through a writing assignment. The camp administrator signed off on the project, and the court granted us permission to publish. Mission accomplished.

But the system was also downright irritating to work with. On another occasion, Mike was invited to visit a classroom at a facility where kids were awaiting placement in juvenile camp. The teacher regularly used our paper to stimulate classroom discussions and writing exercises. On his visit, Mike asked the boys to write a few sentences about their experiences in juvenile court for an upcoming issue of *L.A. Youth*. We followed all the ground rules: strict confidentiality, no photos, only initials for each byline. But when it was all over, the administration suddenly changed the rules. We were denied permission to use the boys' initials or even name the facility.

Libby spent months working with a youngster in a group

home who was eager to write about his time in juvenile hall and his efforts to straighten out his life. She promised his probation officer that we would not publish his name or identify the group home, but that turned out to be not quite good enough. The boy was scheduled for a final hearing before a judge in two months. The authorities let us know that he could end up serving a longer probation period or additional time in a juvenile facility if he appeared to be challenging the system (for example, writing a critical article in *L.A. Youth*). We dropped the story. No wonder that after all these years I'm still skeptical about the probation department.

Seeing the system in action can also be discouraging. On one visit to the main juvenile hall in Los Angeles I was appalled by the overcrowding. Teens slept on the floor in the hallway and jostled each other as they walked in and out. Fights were a regular occurrence, and we were warned that it was a volatile place, and risky to be in.

Brown and Black youth with absentee parents have no advocates except overworked public defenders. They are locked up in disproportionate numbers and often get lost in the system. No one pleads on their behalf for another chance to do right. White kids accompanied by private attorneys were often given probation and sent home to their parents.

The system needs more people like Superior Court Judge Cynthia Loo. She presided over juvenile hearings at the Eastlake Juvenile Hall in East Los Angeles. At Judge Loo's invitation Amanda brought our reporter, Selena, to witness the courtroom proceedings and interview the judge for what became a cover story on juvenile justice. Amanda left behind a stack of newspapers, hoping that they might attract interest in *L.A. Youth*. But we knew it would not be easy convincing young offenders to join our staff. Most teens in trouble have little interest in writing or doing anything beyond hanging out with their friends.

Selena saw a young boy who looked 14 or 15 slouched in his chair. He was charged with attempted murder for allegedly aiming a gun at a police officer. She witnessed a 12-year-old boy charged with a sex offense listen to his attorney and the judge discuss the details. That hearing lasted only about three minutes. Over lunch, Judge Loo told Selena, "I picked up a copy of your newspaper in the hallway, and I want to refer kids to your program."

She was searching for creative ways to redirect teen offenders. "For the past six years," she said, "I've seen an increase in violent crime committed by younger children, many as young as 10. They have access to guns. I see too many faces return over and over again."

I WAS INVITED TO SPEND A DAY at the state's largest juvenile detention facility in Fresno. I spent time with a group of girls who were mostly runaways from group homes and abusive families. They lived together in what was called the Commitment Building, where they attended school, met with lawyers and therapists, and slept in single or double bunk cells. Some were there for only a few weeks, while others might spend a year.

The architect who designed the campus-like complex had aimed for a "kinder and gentler" effect with colorful elements on the outside of each building, but the rooftops were ringed with barbed wire. Not a place for children to mature.

I had hoped that my visit would eventually spark interest in writing for *L.A. Youth*, but these girls had more urgent concerns. "When I'm outta here, can I come to L.A. to get my tattoos removed?" inquired one. "'Fuck the world' runnin' down my arm ain't gonna get me a job."

Three were pregnant, two had given up babies for adoption, and one wept during the entire meeting, wondering who was taking care of her baby. The saddest part was that she had grown up in foster care and wanted a better life for her child.

There were issues of illiteracy. *L.A. Youth* was a tool to help them find and amplify their voices. Voices on the margins. Voices that need validation, "You matter. I see you. I hear you."

I flew home that night with a three-aspirin headache. The visit was a jolting reminder that writing a publishable article is simply beyond the reach of many marginalized young people, no matter how much time our editors spend with them.

A letter arrived from Soledad Prison in Northern California, the sentences childlike and nearly illegible. We had received correspondence from juvenile hall inmates and occasionally someone in California Youth Authority custody, but this was the first time from an adult prison.

The writer, Roberto, was doing serious time. You don't end up at Soledad for stealing hubcaps. He learned about *L.A. Youth* from a *Los Angeles Times* reporter who was writing about him, who suggested that Roberto send us writing samples and become a contributing writer.

We tried reading his letters out loud to the teens to see if anyone could untangle the rambling sentences. We were able to decipher some details of his life—growing up in East Los Angeles, a gang member, fathering a baby, a lost girlfriend, wrongfully held behind bars, on and on.

We sent him copies of *L.A. Youth* along with questions about his prison experience. This, we thought, might be a chance to give our readers an insider's view of prison life.

Letters began to arrive every few weeks from our new pen pal. The handwriting continued to be problematic and our questions went unanswered. Nothing was publishable. Roberto's sentences were laced with attempts at poetry and his professed love for a girl back home.

We were deeply touched by another letter that arrived from a young man behind bars. It was forwarded to us by a teacher familiar with our newspaper. Because of confidentiality rules regarding juvenile offenders, we could not identify him nor learn what crime or crimes he had been convicted of. But his admission that he was serving "two life sentences" was sobering.

Personal stories, first person narrative, placed the writer smack in the middle of the reporting. Our readership soared when we weren't timid about exploring the relationship between the writer and the subject of the article. Teachers requested more copies, letters-to-the-editor increased, and the bi-monthly essay contests received hundreds of submissions.

Above all, the teens were reporters. They learned to use narrative to capture scenes and situations. They wove words to create texture, tone and sometimes, tension. Years later we asked our readers to "Write a letter to mom and dad. What would you like to tell your parents but have been afraid or embarrassed to share?" I was shocked at the essays we received.

Teens wrote about personal crisis, families in trouble, an inappropriate gesture, a parent who drinks or gambles. Who did they think would read the letters? We were strangers, a small group of adults who work with teens and they trust us with their lives. They were the toughest letters to read.

Kids must be so lonely that they write to a stranger at a newspaper and tell all.

# Chapter Nine:
# Of Race and Identity

*On "check one" ethnicity boxes, I was Asian until the 11th grade, when I "became" black. My mom said it would be easier to get into college that way.* – biracial Aisha, 17

I began thinking about race and ethnic identity in seventh grade at Audubon Junior High School in Los Angeles. I was on a lunch bench listening to two girls talk about a new arrival in our class, Maria Duran. She was exotic looking, short and busty, with long dark hair. But that wasn't what interested them. "She's Mexican," one girl said disapprovingly. "But she's Caroline's cousin so we can't say anything out loud."

Caroline was a popular, bright girl, who happened to be white. Her cousin, Maria, was Mexican. I felt sorry for her because I knew she had quickly become the target of racial slurs. But I didn't know what to say or do. I thought about my mother facing prejudice when she was a teenager in a small town in Czechoslovakia.

My mother occasionally talked about fleeing Czechoslovakia in the 1930s to join other family members in America as Nazis marched across Eastern Europe. Jews that didn't leave were arrested and sent to concentration camps. I read the Diary of Anne Frank when I was eight years old to understand my mother's fears.

I experienced anti-Semitism for the first time. Danny Matthews and I were good pals. He came to my house after school, we went bowling and hung out together. After middle school graduation, my parents took us to lunch at a Chinese restaurant to celebrate. The next morning Danny telephoned to say that he was going to a Catholic high school in the fall and we could no longer be friends. His parents had ordered him to stay away from me. To this day I remember hearing Danny say goodbye and feeling like someone had punched me in the stomach. His parents never met me, yet they made me feel unfit to be their son's friend.

I was a student and part-time assistant in a Los Angeles advertising agency when the Watts Riots erupted in August 1965. The impoverished Black ghetto had one too many feuds with police and all hell broke loose. Pawnshops were looted, stores were burned to the ground, fires roared, and gunshots rang through the night. Budd Schulberg, the famed screenwriter and novelist, responded by opening the Watts Writer's Workshop a few weeks later in a rundown building on 102nd Street. He met every Wednesday evening with a small group of writers in the community. I volunteered to edit and type manuscripts produced by the members. That began my six-year association with Budd and the local poets and writers whose work he nurtured. Needless to say, the experience made a powerful impression on me. Budd became godfather to my first child, and on the 40th anniversary of the riots he sent me a note:

> Last night I read your excellent L.A. Youth
> from cover to cover and I felt proud of your work
> and at the same time it broke my heart. All those

poor kids wanting to study and get on with their
lives, and meanwhile obsessed with the mindless
drive-by's and ethnic school fights. It's really so
much more violent than when we were in Watts
in the '60's. And there seems to be no relief, no
real effort to solve those social problems so rid-
den with terror.

As a mother, I continued to witness America's racial divide.
My husband and I had three children, one biological daughter
and two biracial infants adopted in the early 70s when few
white couples reached out to adopt "hard to place children,"
the label back then. When my adopted son John was still a
baby, strangers in grocery stores sometimes asked me, "What's
his background?" A woman once asked my husband who was
shopping with the three children, "So, how many wives have
you had?"

The most painful experience came on a quiet Sunday afternoon, when John was three years old and we were new to Pacific Palisades, a leafy Westside community with young families.
There was a sudden disruption at the end of our cul-de-sac,
where my three kids and a few neighborhood children were
playing in the street. I stepped outside to see a boy standing in
the street shouting "nigger lovers" at my children. He ran when
he saw me coming. Courtney, my seven-year-old daughter, had
armed herself with a toy bat and was ready to chase him.

I calmed everyone down and neighbors later told us that
the boy was an unpopular child with a troubled history. But I
felt physically sick. At that moment I was not the strong, defi-
ant mother ready to take on the world.

My feelings about race and ethnicity are still evolving. But
I know this: watching John and his sister Elizabeth grow up
has strongly shaped my values and influenced the way I view

the world. At *L.A. Youth*, I put a premium on coverage of issues like multiculturalism and bias. My personal experience has made me keenly aware of the conflict and confusion that many of our *L.A. Youth* writers encounter in their lives.

## One or the Other

Biracial children in Los Angeles were required to choose one race over another on magnet school application forms. As the mother of a white girl, a Korean/Latina girl and a Black/Japanese boy, I was tempted to simply toss a coin when making choices. It seemed unfair, as if one side of the family had to be ignored in favor of another.

I appreciated the observations of Jason, a member of our teen staff who was equally disturbed by this. "Affirmative action, mixed race, bi-racial, pluralism, don't put people in categories," he liked to say.

Jason's mother was Japanese and his dad was Jewish. When he discovered that my family was a melting pot, he was eager to compare notes. Jason proudly wrote stories about his heritage and interviewed other teens who were from mixed families. "If I say that I'm just one thing, I'm not telling all of who I am," offered Waunetah, 17, in one of his articles.

Carla expanded on the same issue in her personal piece for *L.A. Youth*. In part, she wrote:

> My mom is white and my dad is Black. In my home and family, race wasn't important—I was just plain old Carla. The same thing went for elementary school. Then along came junior high, a place where differences start to become more significant. I remember the first time I

was ever really questioned about my race. It was seventh grade physical education. Lost in my own thoughts, I hadn't noticed that the girl in front of me was inspecting me.

When we finally made eye contact, her first words were "What are you?"

What was I? Well, hello to you too. "Are you mulatto?" she asked. I tentatively asked what exactly mulatto was, preparing myself for some sort of insult. "It means you're mixed" was her reply. After a while, the questions didn't bother me. It almost became part of my day. You know, get up, wash face, brush teeth and find a way to sum up my racial identity in 30 seconds or less.

The general consensus seems to be that children of mixed heritage are these tragic beings who have no clue who they really are. In fact, it's quite the opposite. I feel so privileged to have a multitude of culture and history wrapped into me. To me, saying that I'm either white or black would be a lie. Since my mother didn't have me through immaculate conception and my father didn't find me on his doorstep, I have no intention of choosing a "race." If my decision happens to spoil someone's survey then so be it.

Alexi also was bothered by requirements to declare one's ethnicity. In part, she wrote:

I can't stand those applications that ask for

your race. I know that they want to have records of ethnicities, but it is unfair to all the
interracial kids who must choose which ethnicity to mark down.

I am half-Chinese and half-Jewish. I feel,
in a way, like the middleman between two cultures. People sometimes ask me if I have problems being of mixed races and ethnicities. I always say that I have no problems with it, but
others may because they don't agree on mixed
marriages or mixed children.

The largest inconvenience I ever have is
being an ignored minority, especially at school.
Maybe, in addition to Young Black Scholars
and Young Asian Scholars, schools should
have Young Mixed Scholars. Or why not offer
Young Human Scholars as well?

At one of our Saturday editorial meetings, the discussion
turned to *L.A. Youth*'s rules for identifying racial or ethnic
groups. Unless a more specific identity is appropriate, our stories identify people as Black, Latino, Asian or white. Not everyone agreed with the rules.

One teen wanted to use "Hispanic" instead of "Latino" in
the article he was writing. Another wanted to replace "Black"
with "African-American." Bad idea, said someone else: "I
wasn't born in Africa so I don't call myself African-American.
I'm Black."

In the end, the rules were unchanged. As a practical matter,
we could not re-write our stylebook to accommodate everyone's wishes. Readers would be confused if we changed racial
and ethnic labels with every story.

CHAPTER NINE

But the issue of how to describe one's self continues to arouse the passions of many of our writers. Warittha,, demanding that schoolmates "stop assuming all Asians are the same," wrote in part:

> I'm not Chinese, I'm Thai! Stop being so ignorant and open your minds more. I want to be known as me. This me who has feelings and morals, descended from a Thai family that has worked hard to make me the person I am.
>
> I don't mind being asked what ethnicity I am or being mistaken as Chinese. I just don't want to be discriminated against based on first impressions. Would you like it if a person points out all Latinos as Mexican even if you were Salvadoran or all Caucasians as French even if you were Swedish? Most will say no.

And then there was Jaime, who didn't want to be Latino or Hispanic, although he most certainly was. He lived in Southgate, a low-income Spanish-speaking community in the southeast part of Los Angeles. Jaime spent every free moment in our office. He attended a year-round high school, on vacation at odd times every few months rather than the traditional summer break. When he was "off track" he would ride three buses and a metro rail train to reach our office. Jaime hated his neighborhood, especially after a group of boys beat him up while he waited for the bus and stole his backpack. *L.A. Youth* was his place of refuge. He changed his byline to J. Isaac. The staff found it disconcerting that he had little respect for his ethnicity, yet we understood his frustrations.

Every Saturday his father dropped him off in front of our

office building at 6 a.m. The early hour made the staff cringe when they arrived at 9 a.m. and saw him sitting on the cold cement. But Jaime feared being attacked by a group of boys if he waited at the bus stop at a later hour.

When he let it be known that he aspired to be a filmmaker, Fred Freeman, a member of our board of directors, stepped in. Freeman, a veteran sitcom writer, spent hours with Jaime, discussing screenwriting and the art of dialogue. Jaime went on to college, where he continued to pursue his dream.

FOR SOME *L.A. YOUTH* WRITERS, religious beliefs were just as important as race and ethnicity when it comes to establishing one's identity. But writing about their beliefs could be extra tough for teenagers. Many had doubts about their faith and rebelled against parental demands to attend Sunday school or church. The pieces they submited for publication had to be edited with special care and sensitivity.

I was reminded of that one afternoon when the editors were reviewing the final draft of Beeta's cover story, a vivid account of her strong identity as a Muslim. I applauded Beeta for the way she had involved others on the staff. She and her mother had invited a group of *L.A. Youth* writers to spend an afternoon at a mosque. Her mother brought long scarves for the girls to wear over their heads, and she showed them the intricate ways of wrapping the scarf around the neck and draping it over the shoulder. The teens were allowed to take photographs before the call to prayer and they sat in the women's section to observe the service.

Her story, in which she portrayed Muslims as a peace-loving people, afforded our readers an inside view of another's world. But I was concerned about Beeta's assertion that the Koran doesn't preach violence. The editors and I debated whether that statement should be published without qualification. Put another way, how much leeway should we allow a teen who is writing a highly personal piece?

Using the internet for our research, we scanned excerpts from the Koran that denounced Jews and Christians and called for their death. These matters are not so simple, Mike observed. "At Sunday School we read from the New Testament," he said. "There were parts that called for the enemy's blood."

"I'll bet the Torah says the same thing, though I don't have first-hand knowledge since I didn't attend Sunday school," I chimed in.

We finally agreed that Beeta was entitled to her interpretation of the Koran. But I couldn't put the issue to rest. That evening I emailed my concerns to a friend, Rabbi Steven Reuben, who led a congregation in Pacific Palisades. His response helped put it in better perspective:

> Now about the Islam thing—of course there are verses in the Koran about killing people, just as there are verses in the Torah telling the Children of Israel to utterly wipe out the inhabitants of the land they are going to conquer and to stone to death adulterers, and to stone to death rebellious sons, etc. and you can probably find similar laws and exhortations in every spiritual tradition. The question is, are there also calls for peace and brotherhood and sisterhood and reconciliation between peoples (which there are in Islam as well) so that you get to choose in this generation as in every generation which passages to follow and which to relegate to another historical period. You either take all sacred texts literally or you interpret them for your age which most people of every faith, including Islam do.

As I write about our soul-searching over Beeta's story, I think back to a brief time when my children were 7, 9 and 11, and we spent a summer in London. It was the early 80s, and the city was bustling, thanks to the impact of Middle East oil wealth. Hotels and restaurants were packed with Saudis spending their new-found riches.

One day as we strolled toward a park, two Arab men in traditional robes approached. One blocked my path. "Is that your child?" he demanded. "I want her. How much do you want?" He was pointing to my beautiful daughter Elizabeth. I grabbed her arm, pulled Courtney and John to my side, and we barged past him without a word.

That night I described the incident to my husband. "Do they buy Arab children from their mothers or snatch them off the street?" he said in anger.

A similar incident occurred some time later. I was frankly relieved when our stay in London ended and we returned to the U.S. I could not shake my suspicions of Arab men. But as I tried to sort out my feelings, I was troubled by my angry impulse to lump all Arabs together. I had spent my adult life dedicated to human rights and racial tolerance. Hadn't I simply reacted as any mother would when her child is threatened by strangers?

I SURELY UNDERSTOOD HOW ABHORRENT it was to not recognize people of color as individuals. I worried about that constantly when my son John was growing up. He had a privileged childhood and attended a high school far from South Los Angeles, where the Bloods and Crips were warring. Gang members identified themselves according to a color dress code, red or blue, with baseball caps worn backwards. Drive-by shootings were increasing, and few teens felt safe waiting at bus stops or walking the streets.

One Saturday night when he was 17, John drove to South Los Angeles to visit a friend. He was in a blue Hyundai. We expected him home at midnight as usual, and when he did not show-up I became anxious. About 1 a.m., our phone rang. It was John, at a pay phone in a neighborhood with a reputation for gang violence. No cell phones in those days.

"Dad, I'm lost," he told his father. "I must have turned right instead of left on La Brea when I left my friend's house." I tried to suppress my fears, but all I could envision was a young Black man wearing a baseball cap and driving a blue car. The combination was enough to raise the suspicions of a passing patrol car or invite a gunshot.

We gave him directions, after which we urged him to immediately get back in his car. "Drive slowly," we said. "And take off the baseball cap!" He was home within a half hour, much to our relief.

My friends used to say that raising children during the teen years were the roughest and once the kids are out of the house, off to college and careers, your worries are over. My kind of worry would never disappear.

One afternoon, John was on the phone. He was a married man now, with two sons. He and his wife had moved into their new home a year earlier, in a nice community in the hills of the San Fernando Valley with an excellent neighborhood elementary school.

"Hey, mom, I need your advice," he said. A neighbor had been provoking the family dog, Akena, through a fence, and the dog was barking non-stop.

"I told him to leave the dog alone," said John, "and when Akena continued to bark I asked the guy if he wanted to meet the dog. Maybe that would stop Akena from being so agitated.

I went out front with her and the guy started screaming 'Nigger, nigger! Your wife is a nigger, too!'"

It turned out that the neighbor, a man of about 25 who lived with his Asian parents, had behaved similarly with others. "He yelled 'Iranian terrorists' to the Armenian neighbors across the street, and screamed at people down the street," said John.

Police questioned the young man but said they could not act unless he made actual threats. I consulted a lawyer who advised John to seek a court order barring the neighbor from his property. It was hard to keep my emotions in check. So many years had passed since our family had been confronted with racial taunting like this.

Three days later, both parents came to John's house and made their apologies. Their son, they said, was "very immature." John decided to go ahead with the restraining order nonetheless, to protect his children if nothing else.

The entire incident struck me as ironic, since it happened on the same day that civil rights leader Rosa Parks died. It was 40 years after the historic moment when she refused to give up her seat to a white man on a Birmingham, Alabama bus. Racism still lived in the quiet suburbs of Los Angeles.

John's wife Tiffani and I sometimes talked about what it was like for them to live in a predominantly white neighborhood. She asked me what it was like to raise bi-racial children, and we chatted about my grandchildren. My Black daughter-in-law and I go all over the map, never hesitating to share thoughts, the kind of conversations you can only have with someone you truly trust. Funny stuff, too. When she and John were expecting their first child, I wanted to bond with her so she'd know I'd be a perfect grandmother. I invited her to brunch on a Sunday afternoon, just the two of us. I thought

I was so clever and cool—I took her to Leimert Park, an old Black neighborhood in South Los Angeles with African shops, men playing drums on the sidewalk and soul food in the local restaurant. We strolled for a while as I looked for a good restaurant. After about 20 minutes of walking around she turned to me and said, "I never come to this neighborhood. Can we go to Canter's, that Jewish restaurant on Fairfax and eat bagels?"

Like I said, my understanding about race and ethnicity was still evolving.

# Chapter Ten:
# Gunshots, Coaching, Bureaucrats

*I live in Watts. Every day is a struggle to stay safe. Kids in the 'burbs have parks to play in. We have trains to spray on. Nobody gives us malls or theaters or any place to hang out and waste time. We have to find our own fun.* - Anonymous letter to the editor, Jordan High School, 2006

I had a hard time recruiting teens from low-income areas. The bus ride to our office would take two hours and cost a few dollars for those who didn't have a bus pass. My struggle was keeping the doors open and searching for money. I got a call that solved both problems.

Thomas Jefferson High School Assistant Principal Roslyn Weeks asked me to train students at her school to publish a small bilingual newspaper four times a year. The funds were part of a large community grant from the state that focused on educating children, teens. and adults on the dangers of alcohol and tobacco. Quite a challenge for a community to confront these issues, especially since there was a liquor store on every corner, billboards promoting the fun and escape from reality, teasers from a bottle of booze and few health clinics to treat the abusers.

Jefferson had been a predominantly Black high school for

several decades serving the South Los Angeles community around Central Avenue and 41st Street. It was once an attractive campus with two-story buildings wrapped around a corner with old trees lining the front grassy area. Inside the front entrance visitors marvel at the photos of famous alum, Dr. Ralph Bunche, actress Dorothy Dandridge and choreographer Alvin Ailey. It's been a long time since such extraordinary young people graduated from Jefferson.

It was an opportunity to work with a group of teens that were cut off from mainstream life in Los Angeles. Besides, the funds would keep *L.A. Youth* afloat at the same time.

## What Does It Mean to be Poor?

I led a twice-weekly journalism program and trained students to publish *El Original*, an English and Spanish language community newspaper. This promised to be an excellent opportunity to share my expertise with students living on the margins of mainstream L.A. By the time I arrived, the surrounding neighborhood had become 80 percent Latino, mostly immigrants from El Salvador. They had fled their war-torn country for a new beginning in the City of Angels, only to find low-paying jobs, over-crowded housing and warring gangs terrorizing the streets. I soon discovered students at Jefferson couldn't construct a sentence in their native language. There was little time nor interest in the local high school.

I met with a dozen students in a dreary bungalow at the back of the school twice a week after school. The campus was empty, students and teachers gone for the day. Sounds of gun shots from the surrounding neighborhood were common. The first time I heard a shot from across the street I dropped to my knees, ducked under a desk, and screamed. The students laughed. When I yelled that someone should run to the office and tell a clerk to call the police, they looked at me as if I were from another planet. "The police won't come unless someone is dead," said Herbert.

"But that shot was right outside," I replied. "Someone could be hurt." They ignored my fears.

"Do you want to buy a gun?" one of the other boys asked me. "I can get you an Uzi for 50 dollars but if you have 20, I can get something smaller."

I told him I hated guns.

The class remained small, only a few students encouraged by a teacher to write for the paper. I had a hard time selling the idea to stay after school after the bell rang.

Enrique, talented at art, produced terrific illustrations if I hounded him. But more often, he sat staring out the window, disengaged from the rest of us. I often wondered why he attended the staff meetings. What did he get out of the program? Enrique spent every other weekend driving to Tijuana with his parents to get his teeth straightened, a cheaper way to get braces than in the states. There were days when he was in pain from the twisting of metal and new rubber bands stretched across his mouth. There was no one to complain to until the next trip across the border.

Herbert and his mother had spent six months on foot making their way from El Salvador to Los Angeles. They set up housekeeping in a rundown building near Central Avenue and 43rd Street. Clusters of adults and children took refuge in the dark, damp rooms they converted into homes, installing old stoves and rigging lights and water. The 20-year war in El Salvador destroyed that beautiful country so families with young children made their way across Central America to Los Angeles. They were undocumented, mostly illiterate in Spanish.

Herbert was a mediocre student. I introduced him to photography. He asked to borrow a camera to shoot pictures in his neighborhood. I trusted him and never worried about losing the camera. I knew little about photography but in my usual way of begging for help, I managed to snare the talented *Newsweek* photojournalist Lester Sloan who brought his cameras to the class and introduced the teens to the wonders of viewing the world through a small lens. Herbert and others found a way to portray South L.A.—festivals, religious ceremonies, murals and much more.

Herbert was a good son. Once a month he stayed home from school to accompany his mother across town on a three-hour bus ride to L.A. County USC Hospital where indigent people wait all day to be seen by a doctor. I never knew what ailed his mother; certainly a lifetime of poverty would reduce anyone to a short life. He and his mother shared a tiny room. The double bed was partitioned with a colorful cloth slung across a clothesline. Mother and son slept side by side in a cramped room with a stove next to the bed.

His mother wanted to thank me for taking an interest in Herbert. Guess who came to dinner? They invited me to dinner one night after the staff meeting. I was served on a wobbly card table in their tiny one-room apartment. The room was stifling, but I didn't dare insult them by asking to open the window. It was probably nailed shut to keep out intruders. The meal was typical Salvadoran, and the most memorable part was the large pot of red Kool-Aid. Childhood memories rushed back to me, hot summer nights on the steps drinking flavored water, sweet punch, the kind that leaves a red moustache across your upper lip. "I grew up in Fresno, California in the hot, dry San Joaquin Valley where sprawling fruit and cotton ranches covered the dusty fields," I told them.

Frank Young, the only Black in the class, filled notebooks with rambling tales of his family's journey from West Texas, selling books door-to-door, hitting the road again when the rent money ran out. His dream was to write a book about his family history, but it took two years to finish a single article ready for publication in *El Original*. He never criticized his roving, unschooled family and proudly carried snapshots of them in his wallet. I was intrigued with his family—brothers and sisters, step-brothers, half-sisters, Native Americans, Black, Hispanic. I never figured out the complete family tree as it seemed to change every couple of years. I often wondered how old he really was; maybe he didn't even know.

He was a sweet young man. Frank was intrigued with my family and would ask lots of questions about my children's ethnicity. It was hard for me to describe my home, my children's school and their lives without feeling torn that I left this neighborhood at the end of the day and drove to a secure, safe place.

Frank was writing a book about his family's history; it was the most important thing in his life. I always carried a bag of fruit and crackers to Jefferson. It didn't take long to figure out that all of these students were on the federal lunch program and had no money for after school snacks. Frank lived with his father and stepmother. When I asked him if he was hungry, he'd shrug his shoulders and tell me not to worry. Months later I pieced together the puzzle of his living arrangements. He slept on the floor of a room, no refrigerator or stove.

"Where's your family?"

"Oh, they're back in Texas. I want to stay here."

I wanted to offer him a bed and food at my house but that thought was unrealistic. My son had bunkbeds; why couldn't the upper bunk be for Frank? Stop trying to rescue poor, neglected kids I told myself.

It was a simple explanation but hard for me to comprehend that parents could up and move and leave their son behind with no food or money. He was a squatter in an empty apartment until the landlord kicked him out. I never knew whether he graduated high school but six months after *El Original* folded, I got a postcard from him, he'd moved to Omaha, Nebraska, and was enrolled in a college writing program.

In 2010 I received a note from him, always upbeat and still writing his family memoir.

And then there was Linda, the only white student at Jefferson. Linda arrived in Los Angeles shortly after the 1992 riots as part of the Revolutionary Youth Brigade, responding to a call for volunteers to join the community in the fight against police oppression. I doubted her story about leaving her Chicago home and school with her parents' permission, to recruit young people in South L.A. to join the Marxist political group Sendero Luminoso, a guerrilla organization in Peru led by the notorious "Carlos."

Linda looked older than 15 and was much more persuasive than any teenager I had worked with at Jefferson. Principal Saldivar was suspicious of her, too, and urged us not to publish her article, that it would stir up trouble on campus. He was worried about the graffiti that greeted him by the front gate every morning—Communist political slogans. He was used to whitewashing graffiti with a gang insignia, but the new graffiti carried political messages. He knew his students were not interested in large scale revolutions when they were faced with day-to-day survival. We decided that Linda was using our newspaper for her own purposes. We asked her to be more specific about her background and the plans of her organization, give the readers more details. She stopped coming to the meetings and we never heard from her again.

DEADLINES. THAT WORD was not part of their vocabulary. Social promotion was the norm, no one was required to repeat the grade level even when they didn't complete schoolwork or pass exams. It was hard to establish a relationship with them since the overcrowded school was on a year-round schedule with students attending school on a multi-track system. Graduating seniors found the idea of attending college an unattainable dream.

*El Original* focused on drug and alcohol prevention. They wrote about teen pregnancy, violence, drop-out rates, and everything else connected to substance abuse. This neighborhood had it all. I feared for my safety, not from the kids in the program but from frequent outsiders walking in unannounced. The energetic principal, Phil Saldivar, struggled to provide a safe haven and nurturing environment for the thousands of students entrusted to him every day. With a handful of caring teachers, he managed to inspire a few students, but more than 50 percent dropped out by the end of the 10th grade.

I was there to teach journalism not to solve social problems. They lived here; I left at the end of the day. Every Tuesday and Thursday evening as I walked to my car in a deserted parking lot, I would say a silent prayer, "Please let me find all four tires on my car. Steal the radio or junk in the back seat, but let me leave here."

In Los Angeles County, there are more than 250,000 young men of color between the ages of 12 and 19, and they are in crisis. They do worse in school and drop out at higher rates than any other group. They attend college at much lower rates than other groups and they have much higher unemployment and incarceration rates.

There are many causes for the crisis. Changes in the American and world economy have made it much harder for young, poorly educated men to get a toehold in the economy. Discrimination is still a fact of life. There are few positive role models for these young men—especially among their peers, which is the group that is most credible to them. There is tremendous pressure to live up to negative stereotypes—from pop culture, peers, and some community norms. A high percentage lack fathers as role models.

Frank, Herbert, and Enrique are now adults. At our last meeting in 1997 Herbert said he had a job with the airlines, he needed to care for his ailing mother. Frank left school without a diploma, wandering the country in search of lost relatives. Every few years I get a postcard from him, letting me know he's still working on his family's history. Enrique—who knows where he is? I've lost track of them. They gave me a glimpse into the lives of impoverished young men of color and left the program feeling as if someone cared about them, their thoughts and ideas. More importantly, the program gave them the feeling they were a valued member of our society.

Ten years later the situation at Jefferson was worse. The anger was raging every day. Fights on campus, boys and girls jumping each other. The police were frequently called to the school to stop the fighting and the only way they can ensure safety is for a lockdown and seal off the campus from outsiders. Concerned parents hold nighttime prayer vigils and peace marches to end the violence. The school district rushed to build more schools in the neighborhood to ease the overcrowding. Small schools might solve some of the problems, but it goes much deeper with rising unemployment and tension between racial groups and recent immigrants versus those who crossed the border a generation before.

We did extensive reporting on school violence in the *L.A. Youth* May-June 2005 issue. Three lunchtime fights prompted a lockdown at Baldwin Park High School. A lunchtime fight at Jefferson High School involved about 100 students, three were hurt. Fights at Santa Monica High School involved 10 to 12 students. A fight between 50 students occurred at Fairfax High. No injuries but several students were sprayed with pepper spray. After rumors of violence on Cinco de Mayo, the L.A. Unified School District reported 51,000 students absent from middle and senior high schools.

We rarely received an essay or letter-to-the-editor from Jefferson students. Teens from the community never attended our *L.A. Youth* Saturday staff meeting or summer writing workshop. We received two letters critical of our coverage of Jefferson, both pointed to the fact that we did not publish an opinion from a Black student. It's true, we only received comments from Latinos. The staff struggled with that issue as the pages were being designed.

THERE WAS ANOTHER SIDE TO JEFFERSON, a small off-site campus for 150 students who might otherwise drop out of school. Every morning at 7, the students met at Jefferson and took a short bus ride to Los Angeles Trade Tech College where they continued their education in a quiet, controlled setting. The tight group of teens were supportive of one another, the teachers knew their names and 90 percent graduated high school.

We had a relationship with these Jefferson students because a dedicated teacher, Mike Dean, cared enough to invite Libby to work with his students once a week. A few of them submitted essays and illustrations.

Few kids growing up in a multicultural city know much about their neighbors. Once, I heard a teen at Jefferson remark that he'd never seen the Pacific Ocean, a short 10 miles from his home. The isolation couldn't be just fear and ignorance.

Teens are disinterested in their own culture, unless it's food and music. High school history is a brief lesson, a smattering on American events and some global geography and history. At many high schools, the textbooks were so old they didn't cover the Vietnam War.

Three years into the project, just as we were making progress and I felt comfortable in the neighborhood, *El Original* was cancelled. Funding came from a state agency trying to tackle drug and alcohol problems. Typical bureaucracy: just as something clicks, kill the program and start something new. The teen-written stories carried a strong message about the multitude of liquor stores in the community, billboards close to schools promoting smoking. The drug epidemic destroyed families.

Today's generation needs the same opportunity. California, no longer the golden state, will fill the streets, jails and unemployment lines with men and women without a memory of success. I've learned how structural racism and social inequity works, not only from experts but also young people at the frontline of failing schools and communities. *El Original* made its early mark with social and emotional learning that highlighted the importance of being sensitive to what others feel and want. The students and I built bridges of trust and understanding. We should have had more time to sustain the project.

# Chapter Eleven:
# Cops and Teens - Can We Talk?

*The whole world was covering the 1992 riots in Los Angeles but our reporters were living it at home. Our voice was different.*

Tensions between police officers and teenagers are a familiar story. *L.A. Youth* over the years published a number of essays in which our writers shared their personal experiences. As you might expect, many were highly critical of police practices, from curfew enforcement to traffic stops. But some end up a bit ambivalent, as in this excerpt from an essay by Ricky.

As a 17-year-old Latino, every time I see a cop, my heart almost skips a beat. I am from an upper-class family, and so I've experienced both extremes in police treatment towards me. One day I'll be walking up my street dressed in some khakis and a polo shirt and a cop will come by and ask me if everything's fine and I might even get into a nice little conversation with him. The next day I'll hang out with some skater friends and the police will be all up on our backs.

I'll give an example. I was at my friend's house in Culver City last year when, at about two in the morning we decided to go get some food and get some fresh air. I walked barefoot 'cause it was a hot night, and my friend Scott took a skateboard. About 20 minutes into our journey (it was about a 45-minute walk to McDonald's), we were walking across an intersection when a cop stopped at the light did a U-turn and flagged us to stop. He got out of the car and asked us what we were doing out so late and frisked me and Scott. My friend Laura didn't get frisked because she was a girl.

The cop searched us for markers. When he found that we didn't have any, he told us to carry on but not to be out all night. He found a pack of cigarettes and lectured us that smoking wasn't the way to go but if we can't abstain, we should do it at home. After he left, I felt upset. He bothered us for no reason. He probably picked on us because he was bored. After all, what are a couple of kids gonna do?

Later, I thought about the incident from a cop's perspective. I saw a whole different story. He was probably just patrolling his area when at 2 in the morning he sees a couple of kids, one of them walking around barefoot. He'd think, "What could these kids possibly be doing out at two in the morning? Why doesn't he have any shoes on?" He could have given us a ticket for the cigarettes or a curfew violation, but he didn't.

Pieces like Ricky's were widely read and served a useful purpose. But Libby wondered if we could shed more light on the issue by bringing both sides together and publishing the resulting dialogue.

"Let's invite some police officers to the office for a round-table conversation," she proposed. "I want real street officers who deal with truancy, curfew violations, busting up booze parties."

## Behind the Badge

In our first attempt at this, four uniformed officers from the Los Angeles Police Department sat down with three *L.A. Youth* reporters on a Saturday afternoon. They talked for hours, and the transcript was so long we had to publish it as a two-part series. All in all, a real success.

We did the same thing with officers from the Juvenile Division. *L.A. Youth* was represented by Libby and three writers—Eamon, Andrea, and Rachel. Here are some excerpts:

> **Eamon:** When you're pulled over or you're being stopped, what should you do?
>
> **Detective Ed Hayes:** When you're driving, you're minding your own business, and you see the police car, and it looks like they're focusing on you, you're going to get nervous. But if you haven't done anything wrong, don't escalate the situation. Like, "OK, they're behind me, I'm going to speed up on my bicycle" because

you want to avoid contact with them because of the consequences of a parent being aware of it.

**Rachel:** What if I gave false information?

**Officer Al Delgado:** A lot of kids we run into—a big majority of them—they lie and they don't carry ID for that purpose, so we don't know who they are. But the thing is that when we confront you and we start asking questions, and you start giving us a story, making things up and stuff, we're going to verify everything that you say. We're not going to let you go until we're absolutely sure who you are, that you're supposed to be there, and you're not a criminal, you're not a runaway or anything like that. So it's just best to be forthright, and give us the right information, especially if it's no big deal, you know, it's just a truancy or a curfew or something like that, it's not that big of a deal.

Eamon: Do police use racial profiling?

**Officer Andy Hanna:** When I stop someone who's driving a car, I'm usually behind the person, I don't know who's driving the car. So how can I profile if I don't know who I'm pulling over?

**Officer Leo Ortega:** L.A. High School is probably 80 percent Hispanic. The majority of the kids that we're going to stop around the school, that are leaving or truant, are going to be Hispanic. ... But I can see an instance where some Hispanic kids would say, if they're talking, "Hey, I got stopped the other day," "So did I, they are just picking on Hispanics." It might be perceived that way. I think through these kinds of forums [such as talking to *L.A. Youth*] we can help each other understand what exactly is going on out there.

**Det. Hayes:** You might live in a safe area that we have profiled as being a high-crime area or high gang activity area. You might be fully innocent and five of y'all are standing out front. Well, all of a sudden two officers pull up and you're not doing anything and you're like "Well, they just pick on us because we're Hispanic." Based on the area you live in, based on the type of crime we've been having in the area, we may have probable cause based on our prior knowledge and experience.

**Andrea:** What do police consider to be a threat?

**Officer Ortega:** Hands in the pockets.

**Officer Hanna:** Bulge in the pants.

Officer Ortega: It depends—different situations. We're doing a traffic stop, and it's late at night, like in an area where there's a lot of drug activity. I'm approaching the car, and I see only one person in there, and I see some furtive movements, reaching under the seat. I don't know if he has a weapon. That's the time I might ask, "Will you step out of the car?" Or I might ask, "Can I see your hands on the steering wheel, please?" That's why it's good to comply with the officer's demands. Maybe you're just reaching for your glasses, you know, the officer doesn't know that.

**Teen photo for *L.A. Youth* article about police.**

**Libby:** There was a student who got into trouble for selling a marijuana pipe and being in possession of a firecracker, which the school police considered to be a weapon. And he was handcuffed and led off the school in front of all of his classmates.

**Officer Ortega:** My partner and I, we try to avoid that type of situation and embarrassment with the kids, we usually walk them off to the police car, and maybe do the handcuffing then as needed. Again, I can't justify the actions of another officer because I don't know his side of the story.

**Detective Hayes:** I want to stress to you, being arrested is not meant to be enjoyable. It's meant to deter you from doing that action again. We put handcuffs on you, I don't care how much you twist and turn, they're not comfortable. They're not made to be comfortable. They are made to restrain you. So, when you get arrested, yeah, it's going to be embarrassing.

**Officer Hanna:** And [the dean] called it in, and [the kid] was arrested for it. You don't take things like that lightly. I had a situation one time where a kid was being suspended from high school and actually made verbal threats that he's going to harm the dean of students, saying "I'm going to wait for you outside, I'm going to kill you."

Some weeks later, another law enforcement officer read the roundtable transcript when it appeared in *L.A. Youth*. He was Lt. Robert Rivkin, head of the gang intervention unit of the Los Angeles County Sheriff's Department, and he was soon on the phone to us. Lt. Rivkin proposed a sit down with some of his officers, who had plenty to share with our readers about gangs and other criminal activity involving teenagers. We readily agreed, but with a change in format.

Instead of the usual *L.A. Youth* writers, the teens doing the questioning would come from Central High School. The school enrolled youngsters from the Nueva Maravilla public housing development in East Los Angeles, a tough district where contact with sheriff's deputies was not infrequent. Libby had been working with a group of these teens for six months, and thought it was important to have their voices in the paper.

The Nueva Maravilla teenagers came to the roundtable in a distrustful mood, ready to challenge what they regarded as constant harassment by deputies on patrol. Representing the anti-gang unit were Lt. Ralph Ornelas and Deputy Ray Bercini. Here are excerpts from their exchanges with two of the teens, Jace and Juan:

**Jace:** Well, I noticed that a lot of cops, the way they talk to an older person, and the way they talk to a younger person, like to a teenager, is a lot different. Like for example, when they stole my mom's purse. We called the cops and they talked to her all night. They looked for them and I remember they had [the suspects] lined up there by 7-Eleven. They had helicopters and everything. They were all nice to her. But two or three years after, I had gotten in a fight right there where I live in a park. I got in a fight, and one of the guys had told us, "Hey, you know, the pigs, the cops!" I ran—I ran pretty far and they caught up to me, me and some other guy. They pulled their guns on us and everything. They threw me on the hood of the car. And this was in the summer, it was hot that day. That hood was burning. I'm telling them, "Hey, this hood is pretty hot." They said, "Hey shut up, and I don't want to hear you." And I don't know what, they just spread my legs and started searching me. And started talking a bunch of crap. They said, "Do you want me to take you in? I'm going to say that you did this; I'm going to say that you did that."

**Lt. Ornelas:** Well, let me ask you a question. Let's say I'm running from you. The call came out as whatever—gang members fighting or two guys fighting. You're the deputy. What are you going to do to stop me?

**Jace:** I'm gonna chase you, of course.

**Lt. Ornelas:** OK, now you don't know if I got a weapon or not, right?

**Jace:** No.

**Lt. Ornelas:** So what do you think you're

going to do to try to get control of me?

**Jace:** The thing was, I would've talked to you. Like, hey, you know, why you running? And just put you against the wall and search you of course. I'm not saying that I'm going to grab you and pick you up like that and then start searching you.

**Lt. Ornelas:** If you seem reasonable, and you know, tell me what happened, "We had a difference of opinion" and stuff, I'll let you shake hands right now and get the hell out of here. When you start running, we don't know what you did. Did you rob a store? Did you stab a guy? You got a knife, a gun? We don't know. It's a lot of unknowns. And the key to us is to take control and then evaluate.

**Juan:** Even though you try to cooperate with them, they won't do that. They won't tell you, "Oh, well, shake hands." I stayed and tried to cooperate. And they still get you, they put you on the floor like that, they put their knee on your back. That's not necessary. Handcuffs, they put it so tight, throw you in the car. There's no need for that.

**Deputy Bercini:** But was there a need for your fight? If a cop is putting a knee in your back, how did that cop get to the scene? If you're creating fights and you're doing delinquent stuff, truancies and all that kind of stuff, that's part of the purpose of law enforcement being on the streets, is to react to that. If we never had to roll to another fight, to another murder scene, I don't think any one of us would be saying, "Damn, I wish I had a murder to roll up to."

**Juan:** I guess they think I'm a gangster or something. Usually they try to kick me out of the park, say "I don't want to see your face." You can't kick nobody out of a park, you know?

**Lt. Ornelas:** Any bad things happen in the park?

**Juan:** Yeah.

**Lt. Ornelas:** We have an obligation as law enforcement officers, to go to the area where there's a problem with violence. And we are going to contact people, and we are going to contact sometimes witnesses.

**Deputy Bercini:** If a rival gang rolled up into the park and saw you, would they go, "Oh, he's not with them," or would they fire?

**Juan:** Well, they would fire. Just because they don't care.

**Lt. Ornelas:** Juan, that is part of our mission as law enforcement. Gang teams, I want them to be seen at those parks. Why? Not to harass people. But to save some lives. Because you know why? I'm 48 years old, I'm tired of getting up at 2 o'clock in the morning and my phone goes off and my wife goes, "Oh my God," and you know what it is? It's a 16-year-old, 17-year-old kid who was shot in the community and is dead. I'm tired of it. And the selfish reason, Juan, how old are you? I got a son too. I don't want my son to be killed. I look at you young people, your eyes, and who do I see, I see my daughter and I see my son. And the last thing I want to do is see any one of you face down with a bullet in you. I've seen enough of it.

**Deputy Bercini:** I'd just like to say in the effort of trying to go out there and find out what law enforcement's all about, you guys should be commended for coming in and putting it out there. I give you guys respect just on that point, because you're trying to find out, and that's what it's all about. We're here for the same thing, we want to hear what the kids are talking about and what their perception is of us, and we want to see that change.

We didn't expect such articles to magically bridge the gap between our young readers and the police. But we liked to think they at least humanize the participants on both sides. That certainly happened when *L.A. Youth* writer Richard interviewed Police Chief Bernard Parks. In the resulting article, Richard admitted that two things weighed on his mind when the interview began:

> First, I thought that police officers are jerks, especially after I got a traffic ticket for a rolling stop a few weeks ago. Cops are out to get everyone, I thought. Second, politicians make for tricky interviews, because they gloss over questions and never give straight answers. I expected Parks to do the same thing.

During the interview, the conversation turned to a personal tragedy that the chief had experienced. His 20-year-old granddaughter, Lori, had been the victim of a homicide. Richard asked the chief to recall his feelings the night it happened:

>  **Richard:** You see violence and death every day, but the night that your granddaughter was killed must have been different from all other experiences, because this time you were a victim.
>
>  **Chief Parks:** It's one of the things that you never want to experience because no matter what has happened since then, you'll always remember the phone call and questioning by the lieutenant saying, 'This is what occurred. Do you have a relative by this name?' Then you hear the word that she is a victim of homicide. Although you know clearly what a homicide is, you have to go through your mind and go, 'Homicide and Lori. How does it relate?' Then you have to quickly assemble and realize the impact it's going to have on the family and how they are going to respond to it and how you're going to keep them together. It is a multitude of things that go through your head, and last thing you have on your mind is 'I'm gonna collapse and just do nothing.' Everybody expects that you're going to be a part of what's going on. You're gonna be giving directions, be a part of it, lead the family, and do all that. It is a horrendous experience that I wouldn't wish on anyone. And it's a daily experience, because you don't just bury someone that young. As a

member of the family, you live with it daily. There are things that happen that remind you of it. You see her mother on a routine basis, and you see her struggle with it. You hear friends and relatives and how they struggle with it. It's a lifelong issue that you address.

Reflecting later on the chief's response, Richard wrote:

I thought that police officers pretended to be tough guys, but he was really honest with his answer. He's still in pain about [her death]. He said that he's haunted by it. It made me realize I'd been prejudiced against him. Finishing our interview late on a Friday in August, his face showed signs of weariness. But he was still smiling in the end. And so was I.

# Chapter Twelve:
# Sex Is Not a Four-Letter Word

*Teens talk about sex. The interesting thing that I've noticed is that there are more virgin guys than virgin girls. Can you talk to your parents about sex? "No, because my mom would think I was doing it."* - Min, 14

Libby once explained in a note to readers why *L.A. Youth* finds it acceptable and even necessary to publish stories about teen sexuality.

"We feel it's important to write about sex, not because we want to offend, not because we want to attract readers with sensationalized stories, but because youth (like everybody) are sexual beings," she wrote.

"Articles dealing with teen sexuality have a place in a teen publication. In this issue, for example, some readers may take offense to the articles on teen prostitution or nudist camps. But those articles belong here, along with the ones on summer jobs, athletic scholarships and music."

More often than not, parents seem to agree. Perhaps they recognize that, in a way, we're doing their job by getting the subject out in the open. After all, most parents shy away from discussing sex with a son or daughter.

I speak from experience. My parents didn't invite me for a quiet chat when I was a teenager. When the nurse sent me home from school the day I started to menstruate, I was too embarrassed to ask my mother for sanitary napkins. I was confused about the changes to my body, yet my parents never spoke a word about it. My fifth-grade class watched a boring documentary, "Where Babies Come From." The boys nervously laughed. and the girls slid down in their seats. There was silence in the room when the lights went on.

*L.A. Youth* regularly tried to encourage dialogue between parents and children on the subject of sex. Our teen staff produced a special two-page spread in the *Los Angeles Times* on the subject, in cooperation with The California Wellness Foundation. The centerpiece was an exchange between Matt and his dad Keith. Here is some of what Matt wrote:

> I was playing a video game one day when my dad said he wanted to talk to me. Uh, oh, I thought. What did I do?
>
> "Matt, are any of your friends, you know, having sex?" my dad asked. I almost dropped the video controller. Oh boy, here it comes. That thing I had seen on TV—the sex talk. I imagined my dad looming over me, sweating with fear. He'd give me some analogy about a bird and a bee and that's supposed to be how I got here on earth. I'd sit there watching him sweat until he was done and then we'd both act like nothing ever happened.
>
> Well, it didn't turn out that way. My dad didn't sweat, and I didn't flinch. He never said a word about birds or bees. He just started

talking to me about sex. The gist of the conversation was that I shouldn't be stupid, something he had told me before, but now it had new meaning. "Don't get some girl you barely know pregnant and use a condom."

I respected his straightforwardness with me. He made me feel like he knew that I was mature enough to handle the conversation—he didn't treat me like a baby.

Moralists who like to talk about zero tolerance would no doubt wince at Keith's advice to his son. They keep beating the drums for one message—abstinence. But Nancy Reagan and her "Just Say No" campaign in the 80s didn't stop or slow the use of drugs. Trying to block something like the distribution of condoms in schools is even less sensible. Anyone who thinks otherwise is simply denying reality.

Epidemiologist William D. Mosher of the National Center for Health Statistics published a report in 2005 that showed an increase in risky sexual behavior among teens. Oral sex, for example, is practiced by more than half of those from 15 to 19 years old. "It's not really having sex," they will say. "And you can't get pregnant."

Not much sexual behavior among teens has changed since then. According to the Center for Disease Control, half of all new STDs reported each year are among young people 15 to 24. More than 46 percent of sexually active high school students did not use a condom the last time they had sex. A sad situation with dire consequences for teens engaging in casual sex.

A doctor of adolescent medicine at Los Angeles Children's Hospital urged us to publish an article about the increase of anal sex among his teen patients. Like oral sex, girls in particular saw it as a way to avoid pregnancy, no matter the risk of contracting HIV and AIDS. We followed his suggestion, and I was pleased that there were no complaints after the article ran. (Separately, a health clinician at a meeting in our office told us of gang initiations where sodomizing another boy was the rite of passage for membership. We were not able to develop that tip into a story, however.)

Sexual identity is regularly discussed in *L.A. Youth*. I am always prepared for objections from the religious right when articles like Marvin's account of "coming out" appeared. In part, he wrote:

> When seventh grade began, and I was 12 years old, I was very much aware that I was gay. It was the little things, such as how I felt when I saw guys in the locker room. I resented being gay and I wanted to think it was a phase I would grow out of. In church, my pastor would explain how homosexuality is "an abomination of nature, the sin that is the worst next to murder."
>
> At middle school the motto should have been, "No fags allowed." People were yelling, "Look! That guy's a queer!"
>
> Toward the end of ninth grade, I was jumped on the way home by a group of boys, who kicked me in the stomach and head. No one helped me.
>
> My mother asked me if I was gay. "Yes, yes mom, I'm gay." She started crying. My mom was depressed. Slowly, over time, she began to accept it more.

One of our most thought-provoking features on teen sexuality was a roundtable discussion between three high school students on our staff. They debated issues like sex education and abstinence. Here are some excerpts:

> **Question:** Where are you and your friends getting your sex education?
>
> **Brynn:** I'm lucky enough, and I think I'm also very rare, that I have a very open environment with my family. I have an older sister and I have parents that I can talk to. But I know a lot of my friends don't have that and I think they get it from talking to each other about it. But I'm sure it comes from movies or the media or places that it shouldn't be coming from.
>
> **Bianca:** I did get sex education instruction when I was in elementary school. I thought sex ed at that time was a good benefit because that age is when a lot of the students begin to learn about sex and hear rumors and begin to have questions on sex. Now, I've been getting my information from books. That's because I'm interested and I want to know. Friends talk about it. My mom tells me that it's good that we're learning this in school because at her time nobody talked to her about sex and that's why I'm here, because she had me when she was 16. Sometimes people are ignorant about this issue because they believe that if you talk about this with teenagers, they believe that oh, you're going to entice them into wanting to have sex and you're going to get them curious. But in

reality, it's education, you're educating them and you're letting them know how to protect themselves and how to have safe sex.

**Chris:** I've actually had several sex education classes. I've gotten a lot of information that I probably wouldn't have if I looked for myself. I think even the kids who don't pay attention get something out of it.

**Q.** What about the safe sex versus abstinence debate?

**Chris:** Ideally you wish that if the abstinence message was there it would work, but it doesn't. I think sex is going to be out there, the kids are going to be having it, so you might as well be teaching them about how to have safe sex.

**Bianca:** I wouldn't buy abstinence. I don't think any teen would buy abstinence, and if they do it's like acting like an ostrich. They duck down their head because they're scared. That's being ignorant. I believe that if a student is going to become sexually active, they have to be well informed. Not just about the physical and the STDs (sexually transmitted diseases) and what your body goes through, but also the emotional part. For some reason, some teenagers take it like it was a joke, but there's a lot of responsibility that can come from having sex.

**Brynn:** I watch my peers and there are some people who hold off because that's what they believe in and they want to wait. But the growing majority of people want to have sex and they're interested in it. That's just something that I think we need to deal with, rather than just blinding ourselves and saying, 'OK, let's just teach abstinence,' because the feelings are still going to be there. I see sex as a big commitment. I see the physical aspect and the emotional or spiritual. I personally would like to wait for someone that means something to me. I don't know how long that will be. STDs and stuff, they're scary and they're out there and that's serious, and you wonder how to deal with that.

**Q.** What are your friends' attitudes toward sex?

**Chris:** I guess a lot of us are horny or whatever. I get the feeling that a lot of them aren't going to wait. But I think it's just one of those things growing up. It's an urge that you kind of have to fight. I don't think any of [my friends] are getting laid. If the opportunity came up, I don't think they'd pass that up.

**Q.** Are attitudes different between young women and young men?

**Brynn:** From my experience, no. It seems all of a sudden a lot of people are having sex and the people that aren't are nervous because they want to jump on the bandwagon. It's funny because people think women don't have as much sexual drive and I completely disagree with that. I think that just in this culture we've been told not to express it as much. But my friends are very open with it. A lot of them already are [having sex] and the ones that aren't are waiting for any opportunity to do it. Which kind of scares me, especially because being a female you have to worry about a lot more than just having sex and leaving and the STDs and stuff, which is huge, but you also have to worry about the pregnancy aspect and being left with a child by yourself. But I still see most of my friends wanting to do it now.

**Bianca:** I have some friends who are already sexually active and some of them who aren't. The interesting thing that I've noticed is that there are more virgin guys than virgin girls. It's so funny because guys are the ones who are always talking about it the most and showing off if they are sexually active. I don't think people should feel the pressure of having to have sex if they're not ready.

**Q.** What role should parents play in all this?

**Brynn:** In terms of educating me for sex, I think that they should play a really big role. Sex is something that we're inundated with every day, images everywhere, yet it's still kind of a taboo subject when it comes to the younger kids talking to their parents about it. I've never really had my parents come in and be like, 'We need to talk' and sit down with me. We have so many questions and we're just waiting for someone to talk to us, and I think parents need to do that a lot more than they are.

**Chris:** My parents have tried to start conversations about it before in the past. I just cover my ears. I don't feel comfortable talking to them about it. I'll blame it on society, that they don't start teaching you about it when you're younger. Had they started to talk to me about it when I was much younger, I'd be more accepting to let them talk to me about it. But it's just really embarrassing when they start to talk about something like that.

**Bianca:** I believe that parents play the biggest role when it comes to sex ed. Parents need to be honest too and treat us like adults when it comes to sex ed because it's something very serious. I believe that it should start little by little. They shouldn't want to give you all this information in one night. My parents have talked about it with us. Sometimes I get kind of shy to bring up some questions. I know what questions I can ask them and I know I won't feel uncomfortable, but there are some questions where I will be shy to ask it.

Some of our writers took a lighter approach to sex. Randy, for example, made a comparison to rides at the Magic Mountain theme park—Viper, Batman, Roaring Rapids, Tidal Wave, and Free Fall. An excerpt:

Like these rides, sex can be fast, slow or unpredictable. Sometimes you have to wait a long time to get on. The rides might make you want to laugh or give you a good reason to scream. It might not ever get started. Then all you're going to get is a sputter or jerk before it clunks out.

My first time wasn't like any of these. It was more like Disneyland's Alice in Wonderland ride. I don't know what ride you're getting on. It might not even be these rides that I mentioned. But I hope you enjoy your ride and that it lasts a lifetime. Remember, practice safe sex.

## Visit to a nudist camp

Kel, who wrote the nudist camp article in 1998, recalled how he had felt ashamed of his body since age 10. Later, he was a student at a church-sponsored school "where they scared us with a lot of talk about sexually transmitted diseases. We thought that homosexuals and sexually active people all had AIDS and we could get it by them breathing on us. And we thought our bodies were something to be hidden."

Kel, who was 18, decided to challenge himself by visiting a nudist camp in the buff and then writing about it for *L.A. Youth*. He tried to lose five pounds in advance of his visit, but only managed to lose two. No matter -- he would not let vanity stop him. At the camp, after preliminary interviews with guests in various stages of undress, it was time to shed his own clothes:

> I went to my room, undressed and looked at myself in the mirror. I said to myself, "Well, this will have to do." I apprehensively opened the door and stepped outside. The wind was blowing over me in places where it doesn't usually go. I couldn't go back—I had already shut the door.

His day at the camp turned out to be rather uneventful:

> In a nudist environment with people of all ages, shapes, and sizes, where there is rarely

a perfect body; you don't feel like you are being evaluated, because nobody can judge you by your clothes. They do not know if you are rich or poor. The males seemed to feel comfortable not having a Hulk Hogan or Arnold Schwarzenegger-like physique and the females seemed content not having a body like Tyra Banks or Miss America.

Kel concluded that nudism didn't have much to do with sex. "Nudity is just being naked," he wrote.

One afternoon in the office, Kel's live and let live attitude regarding people's bodies seemed especially appropriate. I was sitting at my desk when I heard a commotion. The editors were enthusiastically greeting a visitor, "How've you been? You look terrific."

The young woman was heavyset, with long, thick, dark hair and a booming voice. I went around my desk to join in the welcome but didn't recognize her.

"Hi, I don't remember your name," I said.

She was definitely a teenager but when did she write for us? I wondered.

"It's Diamond," she replied.

"Remember, she was David when she wrote for us. We met her when she was 14 and she's 18," Libby explained.

David was now a girl with breasts, feminine gestures, long eyelashes, and makeup. She appeared relaxed and comfortable with herself.

I went back to my desk and took a deep breath. Welcome back Diamond.

# Chapter Thirteen:
# All in the Family

*Tell it like it is.*

I'm closing the door. After 25 years, *L.A. Youth* is going out of business. I have much more work to do, but we've run out of money. Did we make a difference in the lives of young people or change adult attitudes?

I tried to remind myself and my editors that *L.A. Youth* was not a social service agency or a counseling center. And yet, it was difficult to maintain an arm's length relationship with our young writers, especially when we were listening to intimate details about their lives. I wonder if anyone will notice our absence?

We worked hard to earn their trust, and we worried about them when they were in distress. The close ties between us and our teens extended for years after they left *L.A. Youth*. You could say we were like a large, extended family that had its good days and not-so-good days.

Prisco, for example, made us proud. He started out as a

writer for *L.A. Youth*, and became the administrative director for eight years. He handled phone calls, kept track of the payroll and supplies, and took care of anything else that needed attention. He did all this while attending USC and then Loyola Law School. It was a tearful bon voyage when he left *L.A. Youth* to become a fulltime lawyer.

On the 10th anniversary of the 1992 Los Angeles riots, we asked him to reflect on those tumultuous days, when he photographed the violence as it unfolded outside our office. He revisited his old neighborhood in South Los Angeles, and then wrote that little had changed:

> Though most of the burned-down stores have returned, there are potholes in the streets, shabby buildings with peeling paint and empty lots where businesses used to be. People struggle to pay the rent and other basic necessities. For them, the riots are a distant memory. They don't even realize it's the 10th anniversary.
>
> I don't know exactly what the rioters were trying to do. But thinking about the riots makes me more conscious of the inequalities I see around me every day. I just wish the riots had been able to address them.
>
> They let me know when they are living out of a garage without food or money. But that is not all, they let me know when they are proud of their schoolwork accomplishments.

Lupe had a minor crisis that caused us to scramble. Lupe had nothing to wear to the Academy Awards. Lupe, one of our best photographers, was invited to accompany photojournalist Lester

Sloan as he covered the Academy Awards. She had her own press pass, which would enable her to work backstage, snapping her own photos and running rolls of his exposed film to messengers. She was close enough to reach out and touch the shiny Oscars.

But there was a problem. The press was required to observe a dress code - men in black tie, women in evening wear. Buying a gown was out of the question for Lupe. She was so petite that any dress loaned to her by another girl on the staff would be way too large. I had an idea. My daughter's prom dress was hanging in the closet untouched since her graduation two years before, and she was only an inch or two taller than Lupe.

I brought the gown, shoes, purse, jacket, the whole works, to the office and sent Lupe into the bathroom. She emerged a vision in satin, ready for the Oscars after we hitched up the back of the gown with a few safety pins. The next day, she gave the Academy Awards two thumbs down: "I thought it was boring. I stood backstage under the hot lights and none of the movie stars stopped to talk to me."

The following year, Lester invited Carlos to assist him. Lester rented a beautiful tuxedo for Carlos and he had a much better time than Lupe.

Those were the lighter moments at *L.A. Youth*. Sure, there were many tough situations where we had to call a lawyer for advice before publishing a story or a psychologist we consulted when a teen in foster care or homeless was in crisis. We needed breathing room as a staff.

Larry's problem was how to stay in America. Larry, whose tribute to his dying father is in an earlier chapter, joined our staff as a high school senior. His family had immigrated to Israel from Russia when he was five. He had arrived in Los Angeles at the age of 15, and now lived with his brother and mother in a small apartment, in a neighborhood of Israeli and Russian families. Neither he nor his brother had permanent residency status, adding to the uncertainties in his life.

Larry really wanted to be a filmmaker, and you could see his potential in the sophisticated illustrations and cartoons that he did for the paper. We began to quietly scout for training programs that might add to his skills. I called an Israeli vocational education agency, hoping they offered advanced computer instruction, but the classes were only remedial. Libby came up with an offer from the Art Center College of Design, a scholarship to attend its Saturday program for young people. Larry declined, and I could see that he had little interest in any activity not directly related to filmmaking.

As we traded ideas about how else to encourage his talent, I looked at my watch and thought, here we are again, staying late worrying about a teen. It was time to quit for the day. Larry would have to decide Larry's future. He ended up in an arranged marriage, which put him on track to become a citizen at age 19.

Some teens who came to *L.A. Youth* were dragging serious emotional baggage, which we sometimes discovered only when they erupted.

Kate came from a middle-class family on the city's comfortable west side. She had a gift for writing and, seemingly, a bright future. But she was argumentative, always on the defensive, and exhausting to be around. She simmered with such rage that I took a deep breath whenever she entered the office.

When we talked about affirmative action at a Saturday staff meeting, she hurled racial accusations across the room and once argued the need for a "white students' club" at her school. Illegal immigration infuriated her, leading to more outbursts that visibly upset everyone else. Libby told her to stop the name calling. Finally, we asked her to leave.

Her mother came to pick her up, and the two got into a shouting match over Kate's demand that she be allowed to drive the car home. She had a learner's permit, but her mother said the streets were too congested. The shouting went on for about 15 minutes, and we finally had to ask both of them to leave.

She applied for the teen staff editor's job, a largely honorary position that meant your name appeared at the top of the masthead. But we knew she would alienate the other teens and said no. She stormed out of the office, and the next day her mother was bellowing at me over the phone, angry over her daughter's rejection. I finally had to hang up.

Over time, we learned that Kate had serious behavioral problems. She struggled with an eating disorder and tried to attack her mother, after which she was hospitalized for psychiatric treatment. Even while she was a patient, she made daily calls to Libby and regaled us with stories of life in the psych ward.

Fast forward 10 years. The phone rang, and it was Kate calling to apologize. "It wasn't until I went away to college that I really got help," she told me. "I take medication that keeps my temper under control. I come home to see my parents once a year but I'm better off living back east." I thanked her for calling and wished her well.

Howard was a regular at our meetings but couldn't sit still longer than 20 minutes. He would leave the conference room and wander into the newsroom, entertaining himself at one of the computers. Howard was restless in school, too. He told us that his teachers requested meetings with his parents to discuss his behavior. Howard couldn't stop talking and expressing his opinions, even if no one asked for them.

"Museums suck!" he once announced in a loud voice. Libby challenged him to go visit some and share his observations with our readers. That resulted in a piece that, in part, read as follows:

> Most museums suck. Really they do. Museums always have that cold feeling. Very adultish and professional, it makes you feel uncomfortable. And museums are filled with old people, but I've noticed that when there are old people around, it's usually boring.
>
> This summer, as I set out to visit six museums, I dreaded it, but then I'd have a sudden surge of happiness when I remembered that I would be able to bash them in this article. I like making fun of things because I like laughing. When you go to museums, you don't get to laugh, unless it's at the stupid paintings and how much they cost. The artist will put some blotches of paint on a canvas, give it some stupid name, and the painting will end up costing around one million dollars. I don't get it. Why do they do stuff like that?"

I knew that Howard truly loved his time at *L.A. Youth*. He was close to Libby and also liked Associate Editor Sue Doyle. I suspected that his difficult personality meant that he had few friends at school. We seemed to fill the gap.

One Saturday Howard was "high fiving" in a friendly manner. But then it turned volatile. He slapped Sue's hand with such force that it gave off heat and swelled bright red. She demanded that he leave the office, then ran to soothe her throbbing hand under cold water.

Howard walked out and never looked back. No apology, not a word. He was a likeable kid even with his quirky personality and immature behavior. But enough was enough. A few days later, we notified his mother and his sister Sharon, a former *L.A. Youth* writer now attending college in the East, that Howard was no longer welcome at *L.A. Youth*.

Then came an almost poetic letter of apology from Howard's father, a professor at a South Korean university who was away from Los Angeles most of the year.

> I have been worried about Howard in many aspects because he has a rather hot temper and he lacks patience in his work," he wrote. But Howard "loved L.A. Youth" and his expulsion had created "a severe pain in his heart." The father concluded with this: "I think Howard won't ever forget what you and L.A. Youth as a whole meant to him.

Two years later there was a surprise phone call from Howard, asking Libby to write a college recommendation letter. He seemed calmer and more mature; Libby agreed to dash off a supportive letter. All was forgiven.

SHARINE PRESENTED US WITH A DIFFERENT dilemma. She and her parents had settled in Pasadena after emigrating from China. Her mother was a teacher and her father a businessman. The family quickly assimilated, but the parents constantly bickered and finally the mother moved out, leaving Sharine with her father. He rarely bought food for the two of them, sometimes failed to retrieve her doctor-prescribed asthma medicine at the drugstore, and generally ignored her. Sharine shared all this with Libby.

There are limits to what we can do for someone with a problem. We have a directory of community services available to teens when we think it might be helpful. We cannot make direct referrals to doctors or clinics. Deciding our role if we suspect there is a neglectful or abusive relationship at home is never easy. When do we have a responsibility to summon outside help? We have had to go to the extreme of calling Children's Services to report a teen in physical danger at home, but only once so far.

In Sharine's case, Libby lent her moral support as the young woman went through the legal process of becoming emancipated from her parents. When the day came for an all-important courtroom appearance, Libby sat in the back ready to testify on Sharine's behalf. Emancipation was granted. Sharine found a job, rented an apartment, and worked toward her high school diploma. She frequently touches base with Libby.

Sheniqua was quiet. She shared little about her family situation or dreams for her future. There was no one at home to help her. A few times she stayed late in the office to work on her story or homework, so I drove her home rather than let her travel by two or three buses to South Los Angeles. She pointed out a building and I drove to an alley and said good night. I assumed she lived in one of the apartments. I was wrong. Sheniqua, her pregnant mother, 19-year-old sister—also pregnant—and a younger sibling lived in a small room above the garage.

She persisted in leaving the cramped apartment and was given a scholarship to a small college on the east coast. Libby and I asked her a few basic questions—did she have a winter coat, where would she stay during holiday breaks, did she have enough money to travel to college. She couldn't answer. We also realized she planned to pack her clothes and books in a grocery shopping bag, she didn't own a suitcase. We launched a campaign to give her a healthy, safe start. Libby called her parents in Connecticut and asked them to rummage through closets for one of Libby's heavy coats she no longer needed living in sunny California. I solicited friends who played in golf tournaments for large travel bags. We were getting close to Sheniqua leaving for college. Next, the plane ticket. Her financial package included travel money, but she insisted on a long bus ride instead of flying. She'd never been on a plane and was nervous. We rarely heard from her once she left home. I hope she's well.

We stay in touch with many alums. We wrote letters of recommendation for grad school and post messages on our Facebook site to alert them to internships and jobs. Libby is relentless in tracking down the missing ones. When she finds them on the internet or through other means, we send questionnaires asking their whereabouts and what they've done since we last heard from them. We post the replies on our web site, so they can be shared with the entire *L.A. Youth* family.

One alum, it turned out, didn't want to share. Marika was a recent immigrant from Russia when we first met her. She was bright with impeccable English skills but attached herself to teens who were clearly on the marginal side. Marika morphed into Marta with dyed black hair and heavy makeup and ended up being expelled from high school. She eventually drifted away from *L.A. Youth*.

Years later, she responded to our questionnaire with a fascinating autobiography, from her difficult days in high school to her eventual success at prestigious universities. "I graduated from college and law school and that's after being kicked out of my high school," she wrote.

We posted her reply on our web site and time passed. Then,

one day, an angry Marta called to demand that we immediately delete her bio. She did not want her high school misadventures to be floating around the Internet. She reinforced her demand with a threat of legal action, and we complied. That was the last we heard from Marta.

And then there's Angela, who had been one of our most talented writers and went on to be a success in the dot.com industry. When the bubble burst in the mid-90s, she had to find a new way to survive. I hadn't heard from her for three years. One day this email arrived from Angela in New York.

"I'm writing again. Would you be interested in reading my blog and looking at my web site? My life's been an adventure. I work as a dominatrix."

I was happy to hear from her and pleased to read her essays. But I couldn't help thinking, "Wow! Why is she sharing this with me?"

We met some time later for coffee, while she was visiting in Los Angeles. Angela was the same attractive, slim girl with long dark hair I had met 18 years ago. We embraced, and she told how she had become "Mistress" to a clientele of wealthy, middle-aged men whose sexual pleasures were derived from humiliating acts.

She had been feeling spiritually unfulfilled. Yoga classes and meditating on a mountaintop helped, but they were not enough. One day a friend suggested a visit to a Victorian house where women acted in a theater of sexual domination over submissive men. Her life changed after that. She learned how to become a controlling feminist in a secret fantasy world that gave her powerful satisfaction.

Now she wanted to write a book about her life and needed my advice on how to do it. She also wanted to tell her mother about her new-found happiness and career. I silently screamed at that idea and told her not to tell her mother. We spent the next hour discussing narrative writing and books. As we parted, I cautioned her to proceed carefully when discussing the sex trade business with others who might not be quite as open-minded. It's hard to resist my mothering instincts.

Why do they trust me and the editors with intimate secrets? Even letters we receive after publishing a story on a difficult, emotional subject jar me. Are teens really lonely while they hang out with a best friend or a large social group? My teen years are not memorable. I still like films about teen culture—"The Breakfast Club," "The Outsiders," "Dirty Dancing."

At times, there were stressful relationships that drove us to tears.

A white, wrinkled envelope with childlike writing arrived in my home mailbox with a name and return address I didn't recognize. I don't know anyone in Stockton, California, or at the Department of Corrections and Rehabilitation.

I tore it open and found a letter from Eze, a former teen writer. The last time I saw him he was 17. I haven't heard from him in 25 years. My hands shook. I clutched my stomach trying to decipher the illegible words scrawled in the margins, many spelled backwards, two pages proclaiming his innocence on a piece of lined notebook paper. I wondered if he was heavily medicated for depression. He asked for help and begged me to visit. He was convicted of murdering a young woman in 2015 and sentenced to life in prison.

Eze was in high school when he wrote for *L.A. Youth*. He, like so many other young people, was looking for a place to tell stories beyond a school paper. I can't visit him in prison, and I stopped writing. He's a stranger to me, I don't know what to say or how to help.

Karina was thin and frail looking, with stooped shoulders. She trembled slightly. She was fond of the "Goth" look—black hair, thick eyeliner, black clothing accessorized with silver chains and jangling bracelets.

She had been suspended from three different public high schools in Los Angeles. Though she appeared fragile, she had a history of fighting with other students. She was finally enrolled in The Linden Center, a private school for troubled teens.

That is where she met Amanda. Karina was so motivated to write that Amanda couldn't slow her down. The two of them worked together once a week at the school, and Karina rode two buses and the metro from her home in South L.A. to our office every Saturday.

Her first *L.A. Youth* article described her rebellion against a strict religious upbringing and subsequent struggles with drugs and alcohol, brushes with the law, and clashes with her parents. After a fight with another girl "over a guy," Karina was transferred to another high school.

> By then I was totally messed up. I felt nobody could help me get out of the situation I was in. I'd come home smelling like weed or beer. I would leave home and not come back for days or I would come home after my curfew. When I ran away from home or made my family cry, my oldest sister would say, "You're the family's mistake," and "Why do you make us go through hell?" That really hurt me.

The piece ended on a hopeful note, with Karina and her family in therapy, where, as she put it, "we are learning how to accept each other."

Karina was a gifted writer. Her moving story of personal desperation and conflict with her family struck a chord with readers who identified with her experience. She received dozens of letters from teens who wanted to talk with her.

She soon became the most prolific writer on our staff. In a music review, Karina admonished punk-band fans who start fights because "they take it personally when they get pushed in the mosh pit. I mean, come on people! When you are getting into a pit, you are practically signing an agreement that people are going to push you." In an optimistic piece, Karina described how she and her father went to a rock concert together, "an experience that taught me that my father wants to understand me and actually cares about me."

In between these, she produced an especially harrowing article in which she revisited her worst days. Karina described how she had sought comfort by deliberately cutting her arms and stomach. She was told by a doctor that she was showing signs of bipolar disorder, and had her stomach pumped after gulping "a whole bunch" of anti-depressants. Again, it ended on a hopeful note:

> I still have the scars on my stomach and some on my arms. They will help remind me of the terrible life I once had. But I went through it and survived. I know there is a better life coming.

When several weeks passed without hearing from Karina, Amanda checked with the school and learned that she had suffered a breakdown and had been hospitalized. We eventually reconnected with her, but she seemed to be slipping away from us. Karina dropped out of school before the end of the eleventh grade and made plans to live with a brother in Washington, D.C. Days before she was to leave, she was again hospitalized. We lost track of her again.

One morning, our phone rang, and I answered it. "Is Amanda there," asked a woman in a barely audible voice.

"Yes, she's in a meeting," I replied. "May I help you?"

"This is Karina's mother."

"How wonderful to hear from you. How is she?"

There was a long pause and then the sound of the phone being dropped. I heard a small cry and then silence. A few seconds later, Karina's sister came on the line. "Karina passed on Saturday," she said.

The cause of death was a drug overdose. The sister was not sure whether it was accidental or a suicide.

Karina's death jolted us. The editors, Amanda, Libby, and Mike, worked in silence that afternoon, each trying to process what had happened. We had never experienced the loss of a teen in our program in all these years. Psychotic breakdowns, runaways, homeless—you name it, we had seen it all, but not this.

A month later, we gathered with some of the teens to celebrate Karina's life. It was Valentine's Day, her favorite holiday. I bought heart-shaped cookies sprinkled with pink and red sugar. Libby read a poem written by Karina. Cesar read a tribute to her unique personality. "I wanted to put my arms around her the first time she came to a staff meeting," Andrea recalled.

She could barely talk, she stuttered with nervousness. And her hands shook. Larry, the Israeli immigrant, vowed to find a way to honor her memory in film. "Karina was inspirational," Dasha softly commented.

In my mind, I replayed the moment when Karina's mother called, but was too overcome by grief to continue talking. I felt a chill. I wanted to be confident that I would never receive a call like that again. But I knew I couldn't be. So many other young people are at risk of falling through the net with nowhere safe to land.

# Epilogue

riday afternoons were quiet. I joined the editors in eclectic conversations—the merits of the latest music videos, foster care reforms that dragged on without success, cost of college, etc.

"How should we cover the '08 elections?" *L.A. Youth* editor Amanda asked. "MTV will push voter registration and they're probably going to tie it in with a 'green' campaign."

Weekly conversations always varied with political events and what impact it would have on teens.

The mood was warm collegiality as we rehashed the events of the week. I recounted a phone call from the director of a youth center in Vermont eager to start a teen paper. My response was a hard dose of reality.

"Are you prepared to wear two hats—director of a youth development agency and publisher of a teen newspaper?" I asked him. "Call me back after you've raised start-up funds and pulled together a board of committed adults willing to stand behind you when parents, teachers and community leaders challenge the content of the paper."

It's not that I didn't want to share our organizational strategies and lessons learned, but this was not a venture for the faint of heart. It's much easier to start a book club or basketball team.

I'm reminded of how we sought out clinical psychologist Leonard Simon to help the staff through especially stressful periods. It was a sort of therapy only we didn't talk about our personal lives. Len listened to our tales of woe working with emotionally disturbed teens and coached us on how to keep the youngsters on track and productive. "You're touching the lives of young people in a special way, they'll remember you for a long time," he assured us.

The newspaper business was changing. It was a grim picture. Fewer readers, the decline of advertising dollars and layoffs in newsrooms across the country. Cyberspace was the new frontier. Yet, with all the hand-wringing about the future of print media, *L.A. Youth* was in huge demand. Why?

Because we were a necessary idea. Young voices in journalism are so important. It's one thing for a student to read a textbook chapter on immigrant rights—another to read a first-person account written by another teen. Beyond that, I was hoping that youth-produced media would move the discourse among teens from apolitical to activist. We equipped them with the tools to engage in civic responsibility.

Indeed, publications like *L.A. Youth* provided the foundation for a vast transformation. Ellin O'Leary, executive director of Youth Radio Berkeley, looked into the future and declared, "Youth media is at the cutting edge of the intersection between technology, media content and youth culture."

We were no longer the new kids on the block, struggling to find an identity. Print, radio, internet, and video content created by young people combined to form a network that empowered every teenager.

Craig Trygstad, a truly visionary guy, saw all this coming forty years ago. He was co-founder of New Expression in Chicago, one of the first youth newspapers. Craig always talked about the power of the media and the way telecommunications were going to revolutionize the world. He never wavered from his belief that disadvantaged teens would be left out of the equation when the electronic explosion hit unless they learned writing and organizing skills on a computer.

After 30 years in youth media business I still got excited when the bundles of freshly printed papers were delivered to the office. The editors and I chided each other if there was a typo and gave ourselves a "high-five" when a great photo looked better than expected.

I knew that the time was approaching to pass the torch to someone else. I was aware of the argument that it's unhealthy for an organization to be run by the same individual for too many years, especially if he or she is the founding director. The organization becomes too dependent on that person and the community takes for granted that he or she will always be there. The truth is, burnout is common in nonprofits. We work too hard with too few resources. When funding is cut, the executive director is the "glue" that holds the organization together.

I formulated a succession plan in preparation for handing over leadership of *L.A. Youth* to the next generation in a few years. It was the hardest task I'd ever faced.

In 2008, the world spun out of control. The stock market plummeted; banks foreclosed on homes across the country;

people lost their jobs; my longtime foundation support took a hit, and individual donations barely trickled in, leaving *L.A. Youth* in financial limbo. Our office landlord refused my request to lower the rent. The *L.A. Times* reduced the size of the press run so we distributed fewer copies to schools and libraries while sadly eliminating copies to community agencies.

I talked to staff about reducing salaries, cutting benefits, moving to a small office or shared space with another agency. It was a difficult conversation. I called an emergency board meeting. They showed little enthusiasm for rescuing *L.A. Youth*; several members were losing their job and dealing with their own financial blows.

February 2013 arrived with a whimper; I closed the door on *L.A. Youth*. With staff in agreement we made the decision to stop publishing rather than continue cutting the program. I hosted a grand party for 150 teens, teachers and other friends all squeezed into our small office. I even hired a caterer, no potluck. We packed dozens of boxes for storage and shipped the archives to UCLA Special Collections Library, where a single copy of every edition of the paper is available to students and the community.

My dream was to publish an excellent newspaper. It was fulfilled. Our legacy is strong and lasting.

I search for alums. I look for them on social media and call old phone numbers. A few alums, editors and I gather for a holiday dinner in December. We reminisce about stories we published and listen to stories about their adult lives. This book is a record of multicultural collaborations among young people eager to tell the world what it's like growing up.

# Author's Note:
# Freedom for Youth Media

Student activism had a loud voice on high school and college campuses as American intervention in the Vietnam War escalated. At the same time Martin Luther King, Jr. led a march in Selma, Alabama, to protest laws blocking black voter registration while emerging as a leader in the civil rights movement.

It was 1965 and protests dominated the news.

John Tinker, his sister Mary Beth, and a group of high school friends met at Christopher Eckhardt's home in Des Moines, Iowa, to make plans for a school protest against the Vietnam War. They decided to wear black armbands.

The principal objected to their decision and suspended them. They received threats of violence at home and at school. They filed a lawsuit through their parents in the U.S. District Court. The case bounced like a ping-pong ball through the courts, winning and losing, until it reached the U.S. Supreme Court.

U.S. Supreme Court Justice Abe Fortas in 1969 writing for the majority in Tinker vs Des Moines Independent Community School District, stated, "Neither students nor teachers shed their constitutional rights to freedom of speech or expression at the schoolhouse gate."

Student press rights activists felt vindicated. It opened the floodgates for lower court cases involved with freedom of expression.

President Richard M. Nixon resigned in 1974. The Vietnam War ended on April 30, 1975. Activism was out, personal success was in. Students focused on school and careers, making money and becoming high-powered consumers. Few people spoke out on political issues.

Then the rules changed in 1988 with the Hazelwood School District v. Kuhlmeier decision. Cathy Kuhlmeier was the page layout editor of the Spectrum at Hazelwood East High School near St. Louis. The principal censored three articles, one on teenage pregnancy at Hazelwood East, the other on the effects of divorce on students. The court ruled that the principal had the right to censor articles that were contrary to the school's mission.

In 1973 the Robert F. Kennedy Memorial Foundation launched the Commission of Inquiry into High School Journalism out of concern for the improvement of youth's effective participation in the civic and political life of our country. The Commission members determined to focus on four areas: Censorship, Minority Participation, Journalism Education and Established Media. The Commission found that the nation's high schools gave journalism low priority.

The Freedom Forum published Death by Cheeseburger: High School Journalism in the 1990s and Beyond in 1994. The book takes its name from a 1971 incident at Vance High

School in Henderson, N.C. The school newspaper was shut down based on three student articles. One, "Death By A Cheeseburger," was a satirical tale of the death of the writer after eating a cafeteria cheeseburger. The newspaper was closed, the adviser let go, a novice hired to teach journalism without the student newspaper.

John and Mary Beth Tinker stopped wearing armbands long ago, but they travel the country with a caravan of First Amendment supporters anywhere young people are hampered from free speech.

Young voices in journalism are so important. It's one thing for a student to read a textbook chapter on immigrant rights—another to read a first-person account written by another teen. Uncensored student press can equip them with the tools to engage in civic responsibility.

# Acknowledgments

I kept a journal about *L.A. Youth* for 25 years at the suggestion of my friend and mentor, the late *L.A. Times* Senior Editor Noel Greenwood. He urged me to document how we nurtured these writers and artists to prepare them for higher education and future careers. We connected writers with readers. I look back at the impact our newspaper had not only on our teens, but on parents, schools and community leaders. I believe we did a good job.

My appreciation is expressed to those who donated their time, expertise and financial support to the organization— board of directors, foundations across the country, corporations and individuals who believed in the importance of youth media. There are way too many to name here.

I would like to thank *L.A. Youth* editors and support staff for their commitment to the organization with long hours guiding young staff and keeping us going through difficult days. Thanks to reporters, photographers, art directors and production staff at the *L.A. Times* for donating their time and expertise and keeping the presses rolling for us. Many thanks to other professionals who shared their time and talent with our organization.

This book is a record of the young people who ventured into our office to tell their compelling stories. I hope readers learn from them.

# About the Author

Donna C. Myrow is the founder and publisher of *L.A. Youth*, the newspaper by and about teens. She has written about teenagers in the *L.A. Times, Daily Journal, Nieman Reports* at Harvard University and other publications. She served on the California Supreme Court Commission on Foster Care for six years.